A BURIED LIFE

By the same author

FRIENDS IN SOLITUDE

IN A CUMBERLAND DALE

A. E. HOUSMAN

Souldern Court, May 1922

A BURIED LIFE

Personal Recollections of
A. E. Housman

by

PERCY WITHERS

JONATHAN CAPE
THIRTY BEDFORD SQUARE
LONDON

FIRST PUBLISHED 1940

JONATHAN CAPE LTD.   30 BEDFORD SQUARE, LONDON
AND 91 WELLINGTON STREET WEST, TORONTO

PRINTED IN GREAT BRITAIN IN THE CITY OF OXFORD
AT THE ALDEN PRESS
PAPER BY SPALDING & HODGE LTD.
BOUND BY A. W. BAIN & CO., LTD.

REMOTE STORAGE

A BURIED LIFE

I

THE Great War gave me, directly or indirectly, two of the most valued of my possessions: the friendship of Robert Bridges and the friendship of A. E. Housman. The former I might conceivably have won, sooner or later, in the ordinary course of events; we had many friends in common, and already we had exchanged letters, in which my part was solicitation, his guarded but always courteous response. Housman I could never have known in all human probability but for the chance of my being transferred, in the early summer of 1917, to war service in Cambridge. I knew his poetry, I knew his fame in scholarship, but of him personally I knew absolutely nothing, nor, so far as I remember, though *A Shropshire Lad* would come readily into conversation, had I ever at any time heard mention of its author. Later I was brought to realize the explanation of this deficiency. He was to me, at that period of my life, solely the poet, and a name; and his association with Cambridge had never once occurred to my mind since our coming there. I had been too greatly occupied with my own affairs to give a thought outside them, indeed hardly more than to accept the bare fact that we were domiciled in Cambridge, in unhomely but reasonably comfortable rooms with a pleasant look out over the Fitzwilliam Museum.

One late autumn afternoon, while I was still recovering from months of illness, and sat huddled over a severely rationed fire, quietly reading, and awaiting my wife's return and a similarly rationed tea, the door opened, and our landlady announced with becoming impressiveness: 'Professor Housman.' I was filled with amazement. Of all events that could have befallen me, none in Cambridge or elsewhere could have been farther from my thoughts, or if I had thought, from all reasonable expectation. Also none more agreeable to my desires, and it was the appreciation of this truth that served to overcome my momentary agitation. I rose with difficulty from my lounging position to greet him; he was already half way down the longish room, and as I faced him my confidence was further restored not only by his winning smile, but by noticing, from his flushed face and shy hesitant manner, that it was he, not I, needed encouragement. Percipience is apt to be swift and comprehensive at such times, and while he completed his two or three steps towards me, I further remarked his erect soldier-like figure, slight and of medium height, his small but shapely head, the cropped, carefully-brushed hair, touched with grey, and the blue eyes, once doubtless capable of fire, but now rather disappointingly dull — not, I felt, the eyes of a poet.

His first words were an explanation of his visit. My old acquaintance, and Housman's publisher, Grant Richards, had told him we were settled in Cambridge on war service, and asked him to look me up. Almost in the same breath he inquired most feelingly about my health, incited me by questioning to tell the whole story, and listened to every detail with so much concern that I quickly forgot the limpness of the hand I had grasped.

In the light of subsequent experience I can only surmise what this first meeting would have effected in the way of conversation but for the providential provision of a topic ripe for discussion, and perhaps the only one, as I discovered in course of time, which Housman could be trusted to embark on spontaneously, and sustain with questioning and sympathetic comment even till it was worn thread-bare. Not illness merely, but physical disabilities and cares generally, light or heavy, real or threatened, won his immediate interest and solici-tude, and however diffident the inquiries he made, there was no doubting their absolute sincerity: he genuinely wished to know as one confident of the sympathy he had to give, and desired to give. In later years it was my misfortune to provide sundry occasions for compassion. Or sometimes it might be a threat that never materialized, and then, the inquiry made, he would dismiss the subject with the ironic quip and mocking laugh that customarily indicated his relief from apprehension. It was in this vein, the laugh metaphorically illustrated from his vast store of hymnology, that he wrote: 'This is very good and delightful news about your health, and apparently the consequence of shingles!

Ye fearful saints, fresh courage take:
The clouds ye so much dread
Are big with mercy, and shall break
In blessing on your head.'

At this first meeting I did not in the least realize how largely, perhaps entirely, its success was due to the chance of falling straightway on a subject so agreeable to my visitor, one I could tell of glibly, and without constraint, and one in which he gave me every encouragement, both by questionings and by sympathetic comments. It saved the situation. I had been so long unused to strangers, to say nothing of one so distinguished as Housman, so long un-practised in conversation other than that of 'shop', that if, in my then state of health, I had been conscious of the taciturnity he gave me to grapple with so often in after-days, I shudder to think of the pauses in talk I should have been unable to fill, and the tortured and dismal experience this first interview must inevitably have been. From such an imbroglio I was mercifully saved.

He made a lengthy stay, much longer than mere civility demanded, and that, however sparse his contributions to the talk, was sufficiently reassuring, for obviously he was not the man to tolerate boredom. Moreover he looked contentment. But whether conversation had begun to flag or not, there must have been indications of rocks ahead, for I remember the relief I felt when my wife joined us, reinforced me, and amused Housman, with her tales of the long daily queueing for food, and other war-time usages.

He took his leave with a pledge given and a pledge received of future meetings, the former an invitation to dine in hall, the latter the third volume of 'Georgian Poetry', recently published, which he carried off willingly, but without enthusiasm, and which I promised to call for, at Whewell's Court, later on.

Thrilled as I felt by the visit, and deeply as Housman's distinction in talk and bearing had impressed me, I found when he was gone, and while my wife was seeing him away, that my mind was entirely occupied with the sadness of his expression in all moments of repose. I had never seen a face that I remembered that so hauntingly exemplified Browning's simile, 'sad as mortality'. Even his charming and ready smile, I thought, had something of sadness in it, and how quickly the smile passed, and the face relapsed into sadness, as though that were its native element.

While I was thus brooding, and feeling much discomfited, what was my astonishment to hear my wife's remark the moment she entered the room: 'That man has had a tragic love affair!' She too had been similarly impressed, with her too the same thought was uppermost, and with a woman's swift and searching intuition she had ventured the explanation.

We shall never know the truth. But when, seventeen years later, Housman, in the most intimate talk we ever had, told me of a lady recently dead, and in the telling his voice faltered and a look of unutterable sadness suffused his face, my wife's words suddenly came back to me.

Housman's sister, Mrs. Symons, after reading the brief reference to this episode in an article I contributed to *The New Statesman and Nation*, wrote to tell me that it must relate to a youthful infatuation, of which the family had full cognizance at the time, and knew it to have been soon and harmlessly out-lived. But from several statements Mrs. Symons made, she was clearly thinking of a totally different affair, and I was able not only to give her proof of her mistake, but to astonish her with a convincing indication of the lady actually concerned, whom she remembered well as a visitor on two occasions to their home, remembered too her brother's adolescent attachment, but had never for a moment suspected that a vestige had survived the first onset. Mrs. Symons confessed she had no idea the acquaintance had been maintained, even tenuously.

To me, in the same letter from Mrs. Symons, came the flattering assurance of her amazement that her brother 'had ever been able to open his heart to any mortal soul'.

II

Two or three weeks later I paid the first of many calls on Housman in his stark and comfortless quarters in Whewell's Court, mounted the forty-odd chilling stone steps to his landing, selected the door that looked most promising, and knocked. I knocked with a good deal of trepidation. Our previous meeting had passed so pleasantly, and at the same time I was so conscious of difficulties, that I dreaded the possibility of reversing the favourable impression I believed I had made. The former experience had convinced me that if conversation was to be kept going I must supply the fuel, and I too must fan the flame. Could it be done? and done to the satisfaction of such a man?

The voice bidding me 'Come in' came through another door than the one I had knocked on. When I opened it, he was sitting before a table strewn with books bolt upright in a straight-backed chair, holding a book in front of him, but laid it down and sprang to his feet the moment I entered, and gave me the most cordial welcome.

A pair of dumb-bells lay on the floor beside his chair. He told me he used them for ten minutes every morning after his cold bath, and again at night, whenever he felt drowsiness coming on as he sat beside the fire reading. The efficacy of the exercise in warding off sleep he found more potent than any other. He was annoyed to find he had to resort to it more frequently than of old.

We talked extensively of my new work on the National Service Board. I found then and afterwards how incapable he was of initiating small talk, but how readily he gave ear to it, and if the merest tittle-tattle were spiced with a touch of humour or even a touch of venom — at least when its object was approved — how easily, almost as a child, he was amused. He was greatly interested too in the technicalities of the work, the material it exploited, the revelations it brought to light, the ugliness, the momentary relief, the sordidness, the enduring pity. I could speak with both experience and conviction. We were then putting through sixty recruits a day, many of them past middle life, more of them prematurely old — many ill-nourished, deformed in limb, toothless, defective in hearing or in vision — men who had rarely been beyond a neighbouring village, or to the county town for an annual festa: few or none too decrepit, too debilitated, or too forlorn to escape the narrowed mesh of the latest Government netting. It was in all the most desolating and the most degrading task I was ever set to do, I told him, but I was not sure that he acquiesced.

I do not remember whether it was on this or on the next visit that I asked if he were not writing more poetry, and couldn't he hold out the hope of a successor to *A Shropshire Lad*. He laughed, and waving a hand towards his desk, he said there were some half-dozen lyrics in one of his drawers. They were the product of twenty-one years. He might conceivably add to their number – for posthumous publication, he added, again with a laugh determined and full of meaning, but its meaning escaped me, so mocking it was, so sardonic and so evasive. But he seemed very willing to have the question raised, and to hear anything I had to tell of admiration, my own and others', for *A Shropshire Lad*, and I laid the knowledge up for future use.

As I was leaving, he produced from a pile of books on an adjoining table the volume of 'Georgian Poetry' he had borrowed at the last meeting, and handed it to me without comment. 'Have you nothing to say about it?' I asked. 'No,' he answered, and not politely. Then I noticed there was something still to come, and something he enjoyed the thought of imparting. 'Yes,' he went on, 'one opinion I have formed: that your friend John Drinkwater is not a poet.'

I did not tell him that I had reluctantly come to the same conclusion, but expressed both wonder and envy that he could give judgment so confidently, and mildly asked how it was done. He bristled; a dark flush came over his face; and for a time that appeared interminably long, he seemed incapable of utterance. Then, growing more calm, and with oracular impressiveness, he said: 'You feel poetry in the throat, in the solar plexus, or down the spine. Drinkwater's verse touches neither spine, belly nor throat.' It will be remembered that years later, in the famous Senate House lecture, he was to avouch in public the potency – for him the infallibility – of these physical reactions.

III

On looking back from the vantage-ground of long acquaintance, I recall with wonder my temerity in badgering him so persistently about the poetry he was, or was not, writing. He displayed not the smallest resentment, on the contrary he seemed only amused, and, I felt, no little gratified, by my importunities; and so invariably amiable was his response, supported from time to time by the admission that another poem had been completed, that I began to flatter myself they were not wholly ineffectual, and increasingly to find encouragement for the hope of another collection appearing, not posthumously, but while he lived.

When the volume did appear, under the title *Last Poems*, I was surprised to see, in the brief foreword, that most of it belongs to dates between 1895 and 1910. When the subject was first raised, in 1917, as I have already said, he admitted only to 'some half-dozen' completed poems lying in his desk. The assessment was vague, and was intended to be vague, as I well realized, but I was not prepared to find it so entirely misleading.

On one of my visits he advanced other than personal reasons (which shall be given later) as the excuse for his slackness in production. He said: 'People don't want any more of my poetry. It is only a few like you who care anything about it; the rest neither anticipate nor desire more.' He was wrong, and I told him so vehemently. I reminded him of the immense popular success of *A Shropshire Lad*, of the copies that were sold, and still selling, bought, read, and enjoyed by thousands, to most of whom, I added jokingly, I should probably disclaim all likeness. Again he laughed, but the laugh was more indicative, I felt, of agreement than refutation. Mild as the encouragement was, he was obviously in the best of humours, genial and amused, so I ventured to carry expostulation to grounds still less disputable. What, I dared to ask, could justify the disuse of a gift the rarest in any generation, and surely the consummation of all delight to exercise, and however few to appreciate the fruits, to them a life-enhancing and immeasurable gain. I let myself go as never again.

And then he told me what *A Shropshire Lad* had cost him. He reverted to the topic more than once in later years, and on the second telling, and the third, it was the same – a staccato and troubled utterance, a voice striving ineffectually for composure, a tormented countenance, and all the evidences of an intolerable memory lived over again. There was no doubting the savagery of the experience, no, not even though the version given in the Senate House fifteen years later had been ten times more jaunty. He told me he could never face such self-immolation again, and as he said it a shudder passed over him.

The recital, so impressively reinforced by manifestations of face and frame, almost decided me never again to return to the subject. It had moved me to compassion, moved me no less deeply to question my right to exercise pressure. What justification was there for me, the most recent of his acquaintance, to urge him voluntarily to invite the torment he had described, and so greatly dreaded? But when I came to review the matter I recognized how changed the circumstances were from the tempestuous outburst of '94-'95. The sixty-three lyrics of *A Shropshire Lad* had been composed within a period of eighteen months, at full stretch. The ferment, he had told me, was persistent, and was irrepressible. And now he was nearly twice the age, his blood cooler, the impulse quieter, and inconstant, and life was spent in the sedative, if unlovely, purlieu of Whewell's Court. Surely there was little likelihood of a moderated effort producing the ill-effects previously experienced.

The poems already written proved at least a disposition not wholly determined on abandonment, and this, with the amused tolerance he had shown to my solicitations, decided me to venture them whenever a seasonable opportunity occurred. Anything, I felt, rather than have the flow arrested from lack of encouragement or a docile acquiescence in his doubts, irresolution and delays.

At least twice before winter came he gave me cheering news of progress.

I V

In the twelve months of our acquaintance in Cambridge, I was privileged to spend a good deal of time in Housman's company, either alone in his room, at intervals of three or four weeks, or in hall and combination room, sometimes as his guest, sometimes as the guest of Professor Lewis or M'Taggart. I think his taciturnity, or at any rate his determined indisposition to begin a conversation, or when begun to keep it flowing, was more marked when others were present than when we were alone together. But that may be attributed to my own loquacity. The novel Cambridge under war conditions, the incidents of the day, the meeting with new people, some only to be mentioned with respect, some not: these were topics that readily filled the pauses in more serious talk. I made free use of such aids, and however limited my gifts of portrayal, I never at any time perceived the slightest indication of Housman's distaste or boredom. There never was a more willing, and perhaps never in a man of his attainments a more easily gratified, listener. I tumbled intuitively to the conviction, corroborated by all future experience, that to content him one must talk, and keep on talking – the moment and the manner of intervention his own choice; that the silences he did nothing to avoid were an abomination to him. Questions he answered readily, and though in subsequent years he would sometimes talk spontaneously and at length, while we walked [at other hours of the day I usually left him in single blessedness, with a book], it was questioning alone that positively ensured his talking.

Not in those Cambridge days, but years later in my own home, I found there was one time of day when all this was changed, when his tongue was loosened, and he gave freely and faultlessly from a mind richly furnished, and a memory that appeared to have all its store at instant command. His talk had nothing of the entrancing fluidity and copiousness of Yeats' or the scintillation and abundance of Bernard Shaw – and least of all, needless to say, Shaw's amusing, or boring, paradox. Housman's was wholly different. His utterance, like all else he was or did, had in singular degree the arresting quality of distinction. His phrases were apt to their purpose like a burnished rapier, indeed possessed others of the weapon's qualities – its keen point, its shapeliness, its rather sinister steel-gleam and steel-forthrightness. There was nothing of rhetoric. The effectiveness of his talk lay in its fastidious precision – not a casual or unnecessary word, and every word the fittest possible. Interest, and more than interest – excitement – was kept at stretch, and the range widened, by constantly recurring references and quotations, literary and historical, poetry and prose. He was the only man I have known to quote prose, and him I have heard do it again and again, not avouching verbal accuracy, but always with the extenuation 'something like this' – and then reel off a lengthy sentence, perhaps Selden, perhaps Macaulay, or it might be some lesser known author.

The favoured hour, if it came at all, was of an evening, when, dinner over, we adjourned to the library. Except for my wife at her sewing, there was nothing for it but to talk or sit mute, for our guest never once hinted an alternative usage by bringing a book under his arm. But that was his hour, and rarely did he fail us. It was never talk that flowed spontaneously. Stops would occur so suddenly, so peremptorily, it was as though a door banged to, and the speaker departed. In his later and more fluent visits these arrests occurred less and less frequently, and less manifestly; and when they recurred most formidably the merest suggestion, in that evening hour, would restore the flow.

But I shall have something to say on this subject in its proper place.

V

In Cambridge it was Housman's custom, continued, if less regularly, till within three years of the end, to go for a five- or six-mile walk daily, always in the afternoon. The walks round Cambridge are not thrilling: with two, or possibly three, exceptions they are monotonous, featureless, and dull. In those days there was half a mile, nay more,

of town and villadom to get clear of first, and then
a mile or two of highway or cindered field-path to
the nearest ugly village of yellow brick, and beyond,
still more macadamed road, though possibly a
native might know of paths – green paths but little
worn, crossing green fields – where both scene and
footing won something of the feel of English country. Even so, choice lay only between one unevent-
ful landscape and another – until in later years the
institution of buses, in providing a wider radius for
an elderly tramper, made possible the discovery of
a more seductive as well as an unfamiliar countryside. In whatever the gain lay, Housman spoke with
unaccustomed zest of the boon he had found the
buses, and how often he availed himself of their
service.

But the object of his walks was primarily fresh
air and exercise, and these attained I think he
minded little about the scenery. His appreciation of
natural beauty, as with pictorial art, always seemed
to me narrow, unenterprising, and frigid – rather
that of the scientist than the poet. I am pretty sure
he never visited the English Lakes or the Cornish
coast. Under persuasion he joined friends in the
Highlands one year; when later he came to see me
he had nothing to say of it but that it was much
what he expected, and he certainly shouldn't go

again. After a motoring tour in Savoy, in an unusually lengthy letter the chief interest he displayed was for the excellence of the roads. And
always in our walks together I noticed his eyes, like
Wordsworth's, were on the ground: or if raised, set
straight ahead. I never once saw him raise his face
towards lovely shapes of cloud, or turn his head to
watch the play of light and the bewitching shadows
on the upland lawn, or pry into the hedge bottom
where wild flowers — violet, campion — hid in privacy,
and only once knew him stop and gaze at anything
in any direction, and only once to remark on any
feature of the landscape, and that was in 1922,
when the hawthorn, in which our hedgerows
abounded, was more prolific than I had ever known
it, and we were crossing a field entirely cinctured
with its gleaming whiteness, and then he stopped,
and gazed, and exclaimed.

Whatever he felt about wild flowers, he never
betrayed more than partiality, never a touch of rav-
ishment. This, or something like it, was reserved
for the flock of purple crocuses on 'the Backs' at
Trinity, and for the avenue of cherry trees, both
planted at his instigation; but of the latter, alas, he
lived to see little more than the promise. He loved
the cherry blossom, even more, I think, than the
sheets of purple crocus, and many times spoke with a

glow of anticipation of the loveliness the display would one day make – a sight he must have known he would never look on, for his health began to fail at about the time the trees were planted.

Of birds he knew nothing, a deficiency he attributed to the fact that he had never been quick-sighted enough to distinguish one from another.

The one feature of the landscape he was interested in, or at least talked about oftenest and with greatest zest, was trees. Of them he revealed knowledge and observation readily and at all times, but there again the impulse, except in the case of flowering trees, seemed to be their rarity, provenance and peculiarities rather than their beauty of form. 'Where do you find the hornbeam?' I asked on one of our walks. 'Hertfordshire, Middlesex and Essex', he replied confidently. On another occasion he mentioned a species I had never heard of – the green poplar. He had long known of one clump, and one only, and recently he had found another, somewhere in Surrey, if I remember right, talked of the discovery with relish, and described minutely the differences between the green and the familiar black and white varieties. He went on to say that a tree – a lime, I think – found in Worcestershire, he was convinced, possessed characteristics quite unlike the ordinary lime. It didn't appear to be accepted by botanists as a definite variety, but to his mind there could be no doubt whatsoever: the Worcestershire type was the more beautiful, and he greatly desired to introduce it on 'the Backs'.

It is no proof of my conviction that he approached Nature, in most of her relations, more in the spirit of the scientist than the poet, but at least this scientific approach is emphasized by the fact that for many years he had been in the habit of making phenological records. He closely noted the first appearance of leaf, flowers and blossom, and of the variations in season. Thus provided, and aided by an unfaltering memory, he was able to refute and to silence the glib, baseless assertions so customarily made on the forwardness and backwardness of seasons, and the periodicity of hot spells, cold spells, drought, and other seasonal phenomena. More than once I myself fell a victim, and once only was corrected with unaccustomed gentleness, a result doubtless of the correction's coming in a letter. Given in person they were wont to be devastating – a consequence, I always felt, of his abhorrence of inaccuracy in statements on whatever subject. The comments I had written at a venture, I do not remember; his reply dated April 23, 1928, was:

This is not a late Spring . . . there have been so many early springs in the last 15 years that people have forgotten the proper times for leaves and flowers to come out. For 20 years or so from 1887 onward I noted these things in a diary on the strength of which I inform you that the lilac usually comes into blossom on May 7.

I never chanced to meet him walking in the town – fortunately, for it was not till years later that I learned his practice was that enjoined on Gehazi: 'If thou meet any man, salute him not, and if any salute thee, answer him not again.' The rule, I was told by the Master of a College, was strictly and universally adhered to: as lief think of greeting the archangel Gabriel as Housman in the streets of Cambridge; even the rule held in a College court. I can picture him – swift in pace, head erect, his straight line so determined, so set his visage, that to the passer-by he would seem like nothing so much as a blind and irresistible force of nature.

It was during these afternoon walks, while in London, that the whole of *A Shropshire Lad* was composed – one walk, one lyric. To my regret I never thought to inquire where in London he found the favourable environment, or whether the muse was wholly indifferent to the surroundings. On his return he committed the memorized poem to paper, if it were completed, nothing but a few verbal emendations were necessary; if incomplete, the final verse might, and often did, give him days and weeks of tiresome wrestling.

While on the subject of his walks, I am tempted to add a trivial fact associated with them, of which he told me many years later. I had noticed casually that when we returned from our walks, morning and evening, Housman always disappeared for some space, it might be of three-quarters of an hour. It was clear that he retired to his bedroom, but why so invariably, and why he remained so long, was puzzling. He himself gave the explanation, and pointed the moral with vehement conviction. It was his pernickety custom to change his under-clothing after every walk he took. Long years ago he had had an attack of lumbago, and this device had occurred to him as a preventive, and he was perfectly satisfied that its practice was entirely re-sponsible for his subsequent immunity. The under-wear he took off was spread over the backs of chairs in front of an open window. And this, when staying with us, twice every day.

Twice, even on the single occasion when he ac-companied me only on the morning walk. I noticed at lunch that day that he appeared strained and agitated, and immediately the meal was over he followed me into the library, abruptly announced his intention of going for an afternoon walk, and hurriedly departed. He looked flurried, tense and eager, like a man intent on some momentous purpose. He returned for tea long after the appointed hour. It was the summer before *Last Poems* was published, and I am pretty confident that one of its lyrics was shaped on that solitary walk.

V I

One cannot meet a man of one's own race, speaking the same tongue, at an average interval of three weeks throughout a whole twelve months and more, either alone or in the company of his friends, without making some progress in familiarity. And that at least I acquired in Housman's case. He always greeted me with a smile, always sprang to his feet and laid his book down the moment I entered, and however prolonged my stay, never gave me the smallest indication of his wish to cut it short. Except for the difficulty of keeping conversation going, and the consciousness that success depended on my own unaided effort, the hours I spent with him were happily spent; I looked forward to them, not always without a touch of apprehension; always enjoyed them; and always came away the better for them, more full of admiration for Housman, more full of pride and satisfaction for having won and retained the companionship of such a man.

But when all was said, each meeting left me with a disquieted sense of frustration. It was for me an entirely novel experience to be shown friendliness uniformly, visit after visit, and yet never to feel the smallest assurance that I had got an inch nearer to Housman himself. Of course in a sense I came to know him better as time went on; learned many of his characteristics by observation; learned, or seemed to learn, more, and more essential ones, by intuition; but to the last he did nothing to reveal or to explain them, and I had to be content as the mystic is, who adores his saint without requital, and is satisfied. It was as though I had received every encouragement, found the door open, and a smiling welcome, and been left to conduct the interview on the doorstep. It was many years later, to continue the simile, before I was invited in. For Housman's first and last characteristic was inscrutability – a buried life that he determined to keep buried.

I was the more reconciled to disappointment when I noticed how his colleagues fared, they with as many years of opportunity as I had been given months. Few or none of the younger dons were then in residence, but when in subsequent years many opportunities occurred of watching their attitude, it appeared to be rather that of avoidance and awe than of friendliness and cordiality – probably in College, as in other traditionary circles, the customary attitude of youth to age, unless age has retained something of youthfulness. With the older dons the relationship, as far as I could judge, was much the same as among the casual acquaintances at one's Club, perhaps most adequately described as correct – always friendly and courteous, but a friendliness that bespoke no intimacy, no communing of heart, little or no exchange of the things that count for most in life, things hidden away unless something more than friendliness of manner recovers them; and it needed no eavesdropping or personal admission to confirm the surmise, nor could there be much doubt on which side the failure lay. But always he showed pride in his colleagues, and was exceeding proud to be one of them; spoke kindly of them personally, though sometimes with the touch of sarcasm he could not suppress if it could be used appositely, and with wit; always referred to their attainments magnanimously; and of these envied nothing so much as a sudden and painless end.

To this general relationship there was one striking exception – the only one that came within my cognizance, and the more obvious because so much of a contrast. Whatever degree of friendship was attained between the two men, there could be no doubt of the warmth of feeling that existed between Housman and R. V. Lawrence, at that time Junior Bursar. Housman would speak enthusiastically of A. C. Benson, but it was less of the man than of the raconteur, the good companion – the best by far he had ever known – and in all the references, and they were repeated over and over again, there gleamed the remembrance of delighted hours, and exceeding zest in recalling them. It was very different in the case of Lawrence. There he spoke of the man, and voice and manner disclosed more of affection than I ever heard from Housman's lips but once. When in November 1934 he wrote to tell me of the loss they had suffered in Lawrence's premature death, and told of the fortitude he displayed in his intention to lecture on the very day he died, the letter switched off to the unexpected and rather anomalous, but characteristic, comment: 'He (Lawrence) talked so much about me to his nurse that she has written to bespeak me for her next death-bed.' This Puck-like quality he indulged not unusually as a tangent to circumstances he recounted with pain. It does not show callousness or levity, but is a customary subterfuge, and

perhaps an intended disguise, for any regret he felt
deeply.

I knew during my Cambridge days how greatly
he cared for Lawrence, but I did not realize, did
not then think him capable of, the affectionateness
he displayed in word, voice and aspect, when, on
his next visit, he returned to the subject. He spoke
with intense feeling of his personal loss, and the
warmth and quality of his estimation was such that
no man could have desired more of a friend. And
again he told me of the nurse's assurance that the
dying man, up to the very last, had talked of him
constantly. There was a note of exultation throughout the recital; and all he said – words, tone, and
articulation – expressed a proud and glad legacy.

VII

I envied, but never in the early years – nor
invariably afterwards – succeeded in emulating the
few of my friends known to him who found no
difficulty in converse with Housman, who avowed
themselves quite unconscious of his taciturnity, and
whose interviews presented no snags, and were
remembered as occasions crowded with talk, enjoyment, amusement, and profit. It is true that with

one exception all who passed so favourable a verdict
based it on a single experience, in which, if awe could
be kept at bay, the novelty, freshness and excitement of the situation would be likely, unless both
men were costive in speech, to stimulate talk at
least enough to avoid ugly silences. If hours in the
day, and day after day, in Housman's company, still
revealed nothing of his taciturnity, it could only
have been because one of the interlocutors was,
what I knew him to be, the most unwearying of
listeners, the other inveterate in loquacity. In my
own case, for long I was wont to lay all the blame
for the pauses on myself. I was prone to silence,
I was neither nimble nor fertile in wits, and I
found the strain of seeking and airing topics an
inhibition rather than an aid to conversation, and
when again and again they failed of their hard-
wrought purpose, something near to desolation.
Still on my head the blame. Confidence was at last
restored from the least expected and the most conclusive source I could have wished – Robert Bridges.
It was the first time I had seen him since Housman
had spent a couple of nights with Mr. and Mrs.
Bridges at Chilswell. In the selfsame breath with
the greeting he told me of the visit, and without a
pause vociferated: 'Can you get him to talk? I
can't!'

Disheartenment and self-disparagement ought to have been relieved – they probably were – by what I saw of Housman with his colleagues. I had never encountered in private more formidable muteness, and when broken momentarily, a more abysmal relapse to silence, than, for instance, at the cheery gatherings in Henry Jackson's room. The rule was to split up into groups of two, three or four; if four, Housman was given a full reprieve, and not rarely took it in full. One night I recall especially clearly because of the buffetings of fun and astonishment we received. The Master of Trinity was telling us incredible stories of his experience on the Inventions Board. There were places in the recital, if only at the end of each yarn, where I should have found silence an impossibility. Besides, the chronicle was halting, and I was sure no second story of the dozen that eventuated would have seen the light without encouragement, and the last batch not without enticement. Housman enjoyed, laughed and enjoyed, stayed to participate till near eleven o'clock, but contributed nothing.

Such relief as I found in these experiences was rather damped by the tidings brought warm from the event by John Drinkwater, of his first encounter. He had been lecturing to one of the Cambridge Literary Societies the previous evening, came round to lunch, and begged I would take him to Whewell's Court – he couldn't possibly leave Cambridge without seeing Housman. I took him to the door, knocked, and when the familiar 'Come in' was called, left him, determined neither to share nor endanger his enjoyment.

He returned later to give us tidings, also perhaps to display his triumph in a situation in which I had felt it right to warn him of probable difficulties. He had found none. He had found nothing but charm, amiability, friendliness and responsiveness; and the last quality he should suspect in Housman was taciturnity. Could it be possible, of all things, after such an hour of graciousness and animation as he had just passed? Clearly he had had the good fortune to evoke, even in larger measure, the Housman I had found at our first meeting, caught glimpses of meanwhile, and many a glimpse when the conditions were more favourable; but more lasting visitations, more consistent and more in tune with friendship, not till years later.

While on the subject of ways and means to profitable intercourse with Housman, I will here anticipate, and give two instances that occurred in my own home in later years, in which the pleasantest and most affable relations prevailed, in the one case between him and an old acquaintance throughout a long summer's afternoon, in the other with a total stranger, extending over three days of constantly renewed and prolonged converse; and as an onlooker, and not a participant, I felt that the success achieved was entirely attributable to the conditions I have already named as indispensable.

In defiance of the ominous warning 'Can you get him to talk? I can't,' we invited Robert and Monica Bridges to come over one afternoon while Housman was with us. After tea and a brief communal survey of the garden, I left the two men to themselves, purposing to join them only if I noticed conversation were flagging. It didn't, not for one moment. But from our vantage-point it was clear that the octogenarian Laureate was doing the talking. He was in highest spirits and obviously in excellent form, bent on making the most of the opportunity, and Housman's intermittent interpolations and occasional laughter provided the requisite encouragement. They paced to and fro over the lawn as they talked, both pace and talk showing a vehemence of enjoyment I longed to share. I felt sadly out of it, but there was plentiful compensation in seeing the two men so thoroughly happy, and of all I could have wished, those two.

The other incident was a long week-end visit of Housman's when Gordon and Emily Bottomley were staying with us. I had no misgivings about the result of that foregathering. The conditions for success were as perfectly realized as could be: the willing listener, and a talker whose talk, flowing from a full, and I verily believe an inexhaustible, source, could be safely counted on for a mere three-days' needs. Gordon being then much of an invalid, Housman and I went off together for our accustomed walks; the rest of the day, till evening, I left him for the most part alone with Gordon. They sat in the garden, I in the library, and through the wide-opened windows came salutary evidence that all was well. Hours and hours of talk, nor of one voice only, but the other constantly heard in unconcealed enjoyment, and sometimes even momentarily supplanting it, without, so far as I could judge, any pause except for breath. And when Housman came the following year, he referred to the occasion in terms so flattering that I felt Gordon only lacked a paternal Archbishop and a mastership at Eton to vie in his estimation with A. C. Benson.

Long afterwards Housman told me the pleasure he had derived from a visit paid by Drinkwater, accompanied by that delightful fellow, and a poet he much admired, Ralph Hodgson, the author of

'The Song of Honour'. He was glad to meet Hodgson, and was obviously much gratified that the men had travelled all the way from London to pay him homage. But between Drinkwater's two visits Housman's path and his had crossed once more. It was in this wise.

The Times newspaper had printed a lengthy review of a volume of verse by Drinkwater recently published. It concentrated on its plagiarism. It laboured to show that many of the poems were not merely echoes of *A Shropshire Lad*, but adopted its metrical forms and cadences, appropriated its manner, and stole its matter barefacedly. It was at great pains to give examples of both poets in support of the devastating charge.

A few weeks later Housman came on a visit. As we set off on our first walk, he asked if I had seen the review. I told him I had; but before I could make any comment, he let loose his anger and annoyance: the review was grossly unfair, the charge spitefully exaggerated – the work of jealousy, he said; and he continued that immediately after reading it he had written to Drinkwater a letter of sympathy and regret. I could imagine the kind of letter it would be, the balm to Drinkwater, and a corrosive, if he could have read it, to *The Times* reviewer.

VIII

As our Cambridge days were drawing to an end, and the fear of leaving Housman without some associative memento became desperate, I gathered my courage one afternoon's call, took my copy of the first edition of *A Shropshire Lad* in my pocket, and asked that he would write his name, and not only his name, but also a verse on the fly-leaf. After long deliberation and many misgivings, it was to this pitch of extortion that I had arrived. My single concern was to save him unnecessary trouble, and for that sole reason had decided not to beg a whole poem. All I expected was the one verse, and something chosen presumably from *A Shropshire Lad*. He assented most willingly, and when next I called the book was waiting for me, and I found to my immense satisfaction that he had written not only a poem, though a scanty one, but positively one of the 'posthumous' poems, so designated laughingly when he had first told me of their existence. It was numbered XXVII when *Last Poems* appeared:

> The sigh that heaves the grasses
>   Whence thou wilt never rise
> Is of the air that passes
>   And knows not if it sighs.

43

The diamond tears adorning
Thy low mound on the lea,
Those are the tears of morning,
That weeps, but not for thee.

I had dared to ask the boon although I realized
how readily bibliophilic leanings, or many of them,
roused his contempt. He poured vials of scorn on
the practice much in vogue in those days of printing
a strictly limited number of large paper copies of an
edition, arrayed with the author's signature; but
the demand I had made he obviously placed in a
totally different category. It was personal, it implied
homage, and always, as I had already learned, all
such marks of appreciation of the poet and his
poetry affected him pleasurably. I saw he was
surprised, and I felt he was gratified, at my possess-
ing a first edition of *A Shropshire Lad*; and the
book was written in as though for his pleasure no
less than mine.

Once, as I shall tell later, he refused me, along
with other expectant friends, a presentation copy of
his latest publication; and once he sent me a presentation copy without an inscription. The latter was a
reprint, published towards the end of 1933, of the
'Introductory Lecture' delivered in University
College, London, in October 1892. In the letter
accompanying it he wrote:

I think that most likely you have never seen the enclosed lecture, which has just been reprinted by a couple of besotted admirers. It is no use asking me to autograph it.

That is typical, both of Housman's whimsies and his forthright and inflexible determination to abide by them, right or wrong, reasonable or not.

I am tempted to give in this place another sentence from the same letter. Amusingly as it is framed, it conveys the first intimation that he is not as well as people think, and its levity did not disguise the note of foreboding. He wrote:

It is one of my grievances against the Creator that I always look better than I am (as Emerson said of the Scotch 'Many of them look drunk when they are sober'), and consequently receive fewer tears of sympathy than I deserve.

On the eve of our departure, our hospitable friend Professor Lewis gave a farewell tea-party in his rooms in Trinity to which he had, with the greatest kindness and forethought, gathered all the people known to him with whom my wife had worked in the Cavendish Laboratory, or whom we had met socially. It was a delightful assemblage of folk who had befriended us in homelessness, and whose hospitalities had done so much to refresh the lean and rather squalid days we had spent in war-time billets in Cambridge.

Housman was one of the few men present. I don't remember noticing that he made the smallest effort to mix among the guests; where he first sat, there he remained, and there he carried on a conversation with two ladies near-by in convivial mood and evident enjoyment, his face breaking into willing smiles, the laughter both his and theirs.

I think because he had made a late appearance, and fallen straightway into captivating company, I had had no opportunity of talking to him, and on going the round to shake hands and say good-bye, I came to him last of all, exchanged a few words, and walked towards the door. As I reached it a chance sidelong glance showed Housman jumping to his feet and hastening to overtake me. I paused and turned to face him, in wonderment. Evidently he came on an imperious errand. His message, he well knew, would give me pleasure, and the more pleasure from the singularly alien fashion of its delivery, but both his words and the look that accompanied them, though they convinced me of his inward satisfaction, were for my special benefit tinged with mockery and ironic sportiveness. 'You will rejoice to hear,' he said, 'that I have recently finished two more poems', laughed a mirthless laugh, and walked away.

The next reference to the subject came in a letter dated January, 1920, when he told me:

> Last year I think I wrote two poems, which is more than the average, but not much towards a new volume.

The next in a letter, September 1922:

> The book of poems is even smaller than A.S.L., so do not promise yourself repletion.

The last on the subject, three months later, when the book was published, and I had acknowledged an inscribed copy:

> Your generous enthusiasm is very nice, but I have not myself felt more than a faint pleasure in the success of the book, which is not really a matter of much importance. I was pleased by letters I had from Masefield and others.

IX

That I should see Housman again, when I paid visits to other Cambridge friends, was pretty certain. He had not shown me so much friendliness, welcomed my calls so cordially, invited me so many times to dine in hall, on both ordinary and festal occasions, that I should hesitate to warn him of my coming whenever the opportunity occurred. But why I should have felt so confident of receiving him as a guest in my own home, I do not know. I certainly was. Somehow it seemed to me as impossible as it was desolating to picture a future that provided nothing to advance the relationship already existing between us, so tenuous, I felt, but not without promise of reinforcement if the conditions were at all favourable. Ignorance supported my confidence, for if I had had the least notion how rarely he paid visits, and that the house of his Mother's friends, and the friends of his own youth, in the charming Cotswold village of Woodchester, was almost the only one he visited, I should not have entertained thought or hope of his ever coming under our roof-tree.

Letters had been exchanged, and in one of them doubtless I had given him a general invitation, though perhaps not, since the two years after leaving Cambridge had been largely occupied with illness and a long arduous term of house-hunting and removal; and then at last we were settled in the new home, ready for visitors after six years' deprivation, and not a little thrilled at the house, yew hedges, and stone walls we were given to introduce them to. It was at this stage that a letter

came from Housman to say he was motoring to his
friends in Woodchester, and, he asked:

> As you lie on my way, I was wondering if I
> might drop in on you for lunch and renew
> acquaintance with you and Mrs. Withers after
> what seems a rather long interval.

Nothing was so little foreseen, and few things, or
none, more to our wish. It was good that the
suggestion had come spontaneously, and still better,
I felt, that he should sample the hospitality before
being bound to an extended visit.

He came. A beloved brother and his wife — a culti-
vated, well-informed, and travelled couple, and my
brother an excellent talker — were with us at this
time, were delighted to meet our visitor, enjoyed his
company tremendously, and contributed largely
what might else have been wanting, for my brother
had an inveterate knack of furnishing forth
interesting subjects, out of the common, apt, inviting
and fruitful. Housman told me a year later how
much he had impressed him. The talk flowed without pause; the day was June at its best, the garden
less laden than in future years, but very pleasant to
stroll round, to inspect, and to sit in the shade of one
of its great walnut trees; and all was sheer enjoyment for all of us, from first to last. Most profitable
of all, our home had been tried, and found accept-

able. The following year – still on probation, I suspect – Housman came to us for three nights; the three nights soon passed to five; and the visits were only interrupted, once by illness, twice by travels in France, during the remainder of his life.

X

Now that I come to the period of Housman's visits, and before finally dismissing a subject so profoundly characteristic of him, I cannot but enlarge a little on the one and only stumbling-block they presented – his taciturnity. I have already told how for many years I took the blame entirely to myself, until Robert Bridges, a fellow-poet, great in spirit as he was rich in mind, burst vehemently into the self-same charge against Housman. To hear the complaint on his lips, and spoken with such exasperation, so far reassured me that at least I could face renewals of the trial without serious self-reproach.

Still later I was to have a further and more detailed confirmation from the Master of a College, who was on friendliest terms with Housman, and who, before taking the Cambridge appointment, had on two occasions acted as host to him. I chanced to speak of Housman's visits to us, the next one soon due, I told him. A sudden look, half wonder, half solicitude came over his face, so questing, so intent, that it must portend something of moment, but what, I couldn't conceive. Questions followed, and every answer I gave increased the look of wonder, and by the time I came to tell of the two long walks together daily, the look of solicitude passed wholly to amazement. What did we talk about? Three solid hours of the day alone with Housman: how could I possibly face it? How survive it? If I had had the presence of mind to give the fittest reply, it would have been Macbeth's comment on his own difficult task: 'the labour we delight in physics pain'. But it would have been only partially true; for the medicinal effects were not always perceptible, if only because the delight so often wore threadbare.

But the interest for me was the narration of my informant's experience of just this quality of taciturnity, and the astonishment that it should befall a man so sociably disposed, so wide in experience, so courteous and genial in manner. He had found the difficulty of getting Housman to talk so insuperable, and the renewed silences so desolating, that he must plan the entire day in such fashion that he need never be alone with his visitor for more than a few minutes at a time. His professional duties simplified the proceeding by day; when evening came, he was careful to select and to assemble comrades the likeliest to relieve the burden, and perhaps to convert it decorously to conviviality and a triumphant end. He was speechless with amazement when I told him of a five-days' visit, of two long walks each day, and of many more hours together, and unaided.

I had been kicking against the pricks, and blaming myself for the ineffectual results. The testimony of these two men – a Poet Laureate and the Master of a famous College – had it come sooner, might not have lessened my persistence, but it would have made failure more comfortable because inevitable, and left unaffected the last infirmity of wonted mind.

In retrospect it is hard, if not impossible, to believe the struggle I found it to keep conversation going, and this particularly during the earlier visits, and always most difficult on the morning walk. The pleasures of life are so much more vividly recalled, so much less questionable than its ills and exactions, all of which save the heaviest are remembered, if at all, only as the dry bones that no effort of imagination will reclothe with sentient flesh. What lives and has its being now – and all else is counted nothing – is my growing affection and intense and deepening admiration for Housman, my

pride in his friendship, my profit in his companionship, the happiness he brought me, the kindnesses
he did me, and, as a crowning boon, the exceeding
pleasure of noting the growth in intimacy, and his
reticence and concealment gradually thinning like
an autumn mist, to reveal something of the secrets
they had hidden.

But remembered facts there is no blinking, and
when I recall my state at the end of the earlier
visits, and the feeling of relief with which I speeded
him away, despite the sense of loss, there cannot be
any doubt of the strain involved. When at home,
until dinner came, Housman was left to his own
devices; either in the garden or the library he read
his own book or one from my shelves; and always
after breakfast, and again in the evening, he would
wander to and fro along the herbaceous border, and
I would often see him stoop low to win some
fragrance, or, to the same end, tread stealthily
across the border till he reached the hindmost row,
and there bury his face in a truss of bloom. It was
the scent that seemed to give him special delight,
and was always his first quest when he came upon
a flower unknown to him. And his black wrath
when he found a new variety had been gained at
the sacrifice of the fragrance possessed by its parent
stock!

The tour of the garden over, I joined him, and we set off on our five- or six-mile tramp, he absurdly equipped for rough walking with elastic-side boots and a genteel silver-knobbed ebony stick; though doubtless, as I often felt, my own equipment for the project was still more inadequate. It was nothing less than an unaided effort to keep conversation flowing. When one searching inquiry had satisfied him about my health, or perhaps some other personal care recollected from a previous visit – and these things he never delayed to ask, and asked peremptorily – it might be that he would not make a single spontaneous remark throughout the walk. A June morning, radiant and replenishing, and not a word of acknowledgment, not a breath of thanksgiving, but all its tidings falling as it were on deaf ears! If there was to be talk I must look entirely to his responsiveness to the subjects I raised. It was the parable of the sower in grim earnest: 'Some fell by the wayside . . . some fell upon stony places, where they had not much earth . . . and some fell among thorns.' This was the fate of many a morning walk, and repeated more or less inexorably in the evening. But not always, and far less frequently in later years; but always until the hour of deliverance that came after dinner, the sowing had to be done, and then of the seed others fell into good ground, 'brought forth fruit, some an hundred-fold, some sixty-fold, some thirty-fold'. In the lusty sowings of the early years I was still content with less, with twenty- nay, even with five-fold.

Sometimes it would happen during the morning walk that he was morose and ill-tempered, a state I attributed to physical causes, and for which I could make every allowance, save on the few occasions when it found physical expression, and, one of the dogs crossing his path, he would lunge out with a foot, and appeared to derive satisfaction if the mean assault were effectual. Those mornings were the most difficult.

We overtook our village children in the lanes, fresh and comely little maidens mothering, perhaps, an infant in a perambulator, or gathering wild flowers, or shyly stopping to look at us as we passed. I should never have supposed he was conscious of their presence but for the fact that his eyes were more resolutely set forward. The shepherds and labourers on the land were all my friends, and half the pleasure of a walk, as Scott found on Tweedside, was to have a 'crack' with them. I stopped one morning to exchange a few words with one who would wait for me two fields away, a fellow full to the brim of country lore. As we approached him I told Housman how good a fellow he was, how wise,

and that I must stop for a moment. I supposed
Housman also would stop. Surely a poet who had
sung so passionately the theme of a Shropshire lad
would be interested in a passing word with his Ox-
fordshire exemplar. I was mistaken. He walked
steadily on, as though the lane were vacant, and
when a few minutes later I overtook him, his face
was clouded with – was it merely annoyance, or was
it superciliousness? I don't know; it was glum
enough for either.

X I

An American author wrote to me to ask what
Housman talked about while we walked, and particularly whether he made any comments on the
country we passed through, and on what special
features of it. In a later letter he asked details of
his toilette, of his routine practices, of the clothes he
wore in the country; did he walk with a stick or an
umbrella, what newspapers he read, what other
reading he did on holiday, and much else. So much
that, had I kept the letters, the ground would have
been so thoroughly prepared, that these recollections had needed only discretion in the assembling,
and lost nothing from failure of guidance.

My correspondent went on to say that he had once called on Housman in Whewell's Court. He was, I should guess, a voluble talker, uninhibited by diffidence, spurred by curiosity, and thrilled by a vaunted presence; he had come moreover to pay homage, and homage, if it were discreet, Housman, like other poets, was not indifferent to. So all went well. The visitor was delighted with his interview. He found Housman charming, so affable, genial, the very soul of companionableness – all, in short, so much the reverse of the Housman on a five-mile morning walk.

The choice lay between bleak silences and a constantly renewed effort to find subjects that would draw something more than a chilling and the briefest possible comment. There were some I quickly learned to avoid, like humanitarianism. One, he himself warned me off, when I innocently put some question in metaphysics – something, if I remember right, about 'all this unintelligible world' – and he replied angrily: 'that is a subject I will not discuss!' His objection apparently to the whole realm of philosophic thought was indicated later by the withering contempt with which he referred incidentally to the scheme of immortality that 'appeared to satisfy' his colleague M'Taggart. Strange, I thought, in a man of Housman's attainments to bang the door, and shut himself out from one of the most spacious of all intellectual enterprises. But if this mine was closed, there were many others, and ore in plenty. It was my business to detect as much of it as was within my reach, and to bring it to the surface.

In the main we discussed literary subjects, and more especially English poetry. He was not very easy to draw on the question of contemporary poets. He disliked 'free verse', and found little or nothing in it of the qualities he sought in poetry. Referring to *The Testament of Beauty*, he said, 'Bridges does not send me much of his new-fangled stuff, because he has given up hopes of converting me to it'. Nor did he care greatly for most of Bridges' later work, but he was enthusiastic in his praise of the *Shorter Poems*, as first published in 1890, comprising Books I-IV. The lyrics in Book V, printed later with the others in the private press of H. Daniel, he thought nothing like so good. Of the four books issued in 1890, he said that probably no single volume of English verse had ever maintained such perfection; and he went on to speak of the immense difficulty anthologists of the future would find in making a selection. William Watson's poem, 'Wordsworth's Grave', I was delighted to hear him pronounce 'one of the precious things in our literature'. He spoke in warm praise of Ralph Hodgson's 'Song of Honour', adding, 'Yes, but what a debt it owes to Smart's "Song to David"!' Margaret Woods he placed with Christina Rossetti and Alice Meynell as our three best women poets. I was a little surprised to hear his partiality for Francis Thompson, and for so much of his work. He greatly admired Bridges' essays in criticism, while so strongly resenting his opinions on many of our poets. His attitude towards Gerard Hopkins he looked on as a personal foible.

It flattered me to note how largely our opinions coincided, almost invariably, I think, in general estimation, both of poets and individual poems, if not always in degree; and it was a profound satisfaction to hear his approval of the work of some of my friends, for instance, Lascelles Abercrombie, much of John Masefield, and many of the lyrics of Walter de la Mare. To Masefield, of whom we talked many times, he evidently owed more of those physical reactions in solar plexus, throat, and spine, than to any other living poet, and his only stricture on de la Mare's poems was, that the rich promise usual in the openings was not always infallibly realized, and having excited expectation, left a feeling of disappointment, even though no serious charge could be brought against the ending on its own merits. Of Abercrombie he said little, but always referred to him with admiration and the greatest respect, comparing him with Browning for searching imagination, potent imagery and intellectual force; and I couldn't resist the belief that he too, like Alice Meynell, who affirmed it with conviction, placed him among the immortals.

Shelley, he thought, maintained a higher standard of excellence than all other English poets; no lapses in him so stark or so bewildering as those to be found — to go no further back than last century — in Byron, Tennyson, Browning, Arnold, Swinburne; nothing so tiresome as most of Wordsworth's outpourings from Rydal Mount. Though from incidental remarks I should infer that he exalted Wordsworth to much the same position as had been given him in 'Essays in Criticism'. He spoke of his preference, with something of the reluctance of loyalty, I felt, for 'The Prelude' to 'The Excursion', and averred with warmth that many of its passages were among Wordsworth's best. High among the lyrics, and very high, he put 'The Leech-Gatherer' — so high that I could not but wonder whether an instinctive predilection for narrative, so markedly exemplified in *A Shropshire Lad*, and in many poems he chose for special praise, was not a factor in his partiality.

Like all other readers, not poets only, with any pretension to discrimination and taste, he had a great admiration for Coventry Patmore's *Odes*; while his praises for Browning and Matthew Arnold were such as led me to presume that he won greater enjoyment out of much more of both men's work than Tennyson's.

X I I

The English Muse provided an excellent touchstone to the scale and efficiency of his critical apparatus – his abounding knowledge, his exquisite sensibility, fastidious but catholic taste, fine discrimination, and sane and unprejudiced judgment. If he did not possess each of these qualities in greater measure than others of my literary friends, they were in him so perfectly combined and so scrupulously disciplined, that I should have felt more confidence in an assessment of his than in that of any living man.

On one of our walks a comparison – and a contrast – was instituted by Housman's telling me that the Poet Laureate had consulted him on many questions about the anthology he was preparing,

The Chilswell Book of English Poetry. Robert
Bridges was so revered a friend, so greatly admired,
and so beloved that I should not willingly have
brought him, least of all to his disadvantage, in
comparison even with Housman. But he is big
enough in stature to lose nothing of it even though
all his limitations, faults and foibles were set forth.
And probably the making of an anthology would
best expose them. For he was full of whimsies.
With that great guffaw of his – Olympian like all else
of him – he would ruthlessly sweep away not one,
but many of the fixed stars in our national galaxy.
He had, to my own knowledge, blind – totally blind
– spots for Dryden, Browning, and Arnold, and saw
Wordsworth as it were through a glass darkly, while
favouring so much lesser men like Hopkins and
Andrew Lang, both, I suspect, primarily from personal attachment. Housman far from approved the
choice of many poems in the Chilswell anthology,
and suggested alternatives; but he was positively
shocked to find that, as a consequence of the blind
spots, no place had been found for, among others,
either Matthew Arnold or Browning. He insisted
that no reputable anthology could possibly be given
to the English reader, and most unpardonably of all
to the youthful reader, with those two names ex-
cluded. Bridges gave way to the extent of admitting

both poets, but in what spirit, the examples selected sufficiently indicate.

Our talks ranged over other fields than literature. There were few subjects I was not eager to hear him discuss, and so I cast my net far and wide, and rarely failed of some valuable catch. The tiresome efforts and the constant failures of the early visits grew less, till on the last three or four I had the satisfaction of seeing them almost completely gone. How the change came about is no matter. All I desired of it, and so much more than I had believed possible, I got. It came so effectually – I could not but feel so miraculously – that on many of our walks it was Housman who talked, I doing nothing beyond an interpolation of acquiescence or question, and taking all the rich gain.

It was a chance remark on one of our evening walks that led to Housman's most prolonged and most entertaining monologue, though not the one I treasure most in memory. I had recently spent the inside of a week in Cambridge, and dining one night at Caius had been specially introduced to a classical don as being one of Housman's fervid admirers. Such he proved to be; and we spent the long evening in closest and aloof converse, Housman the sole topic, exchanging memories, and mutually warmed by an experience, the first that had befallen me so bountifully in Cambridge or elsewhere. In the course of conversation he referred to Housman as our greatest classical scholar since Bentley.

This was not the first time I had heard the opinion expressed, and I repeated it guilelessly to Housman when he had come to an end of his pyrotechnic display of memory in detailing the heights of the towers or spires, and of the naves of some score of English and French cathedrals. The effect was unsuspected. He suddenly stopped dead, his face darkened, and he betrayed all the signs of agitation I had come to associate with him on occasion, but never witnessed in others, man or woman. For a few moments I was left in perplexity, and when at last words came they were spoken angrily. 'I will not tolerate comparison with Bentley,' he said. 'Bentley is alone and supreme. They may compare me with Porson if they will – the comparison is not preposterous – he surpassed me in some qualities as I claim to surpass him in others.' He gave one example where he considered he held the advantage, but, alas, I had been too perturbed in spirit to retain the statement, or perhaps it was that the racy talk immediately following put it clean out of my head. I regret the loss, but for me is the plenteous compensation of an hour's talk on the two eighteenth-century scholars, enjoyed I think equally by talker and listener, in which Housman told of both effectively, and of Porson a long series of delicious anecdotes.

XIII

Of all the subjects of our talks none gave me so much satisfaction as Housman's story of *A Shropshire Lad* – its incipience, the time and the manner of composition, what the progress and what the delays, and indeed whatever he was willing to tell. And always he seemed very willing, so much so that he gave me the impression of wishing to hide nothing. He volunteered information as readily as he answered questions. Most of the facts I got in two conversations, and in one of them he reverted spontaneously to the cost entailed, and again the pained look showed only too clearly how heavy it had been, and with what bitterness the memory was recalled after all these years.

He had written light verse in youth for the amusement of his brothers and sisters, and later he wove verses for his own amusement while dressing in the morning, a practice he certainly continued until 1922, when he included a topical specimen in a letter to me. Till then I knew nothing of the habit. I wrote at once to tell him the immense pleasure it had given me to receive so finished and excellent a

E

verse in a morning letter, and to thank him. I said how my appetite was whetted. But thanks and importunities were alike in vain, and the one example of his by-play skill had to suffice me. The letter containing it was written during the election of a Pope, and after telling me: 'No, no more poetry, or at least nothing to speak of', he concludes:

> 'It is a fearful thing to be
>   The Pope.
> That cross will not be laid on me,
>   I hope.
> A righteous God would not permit
>   It.
> The Pope himself must often say,
> After the labours of the day,
> "It is a fearful thing to be
>   Me".'

But to the best of my belief, and indeed his own word could only be taken to imply confirmation, he had never attempted serious verse until he definitely embarked on the *Shropshire Lad* poems. He said his preparation for this venture was a long concentrated course of study and thought – precisely the devices, I suppose, he brought so effectually to his textual work – and that he did nothing by way of practising the technique of verse writing. When I asked him whether he had been influenced by any of the other poets, he promptly replied: Yes, he had taken as models the *Border Ballads*, Shakespeare's *Songs*, and Heine. He had carefully – I inferred from his statement, almost meticulously – investigated all three sources, though equally he had been careful to avoid imitation: they had been no more, he believed, than fortunate influences. The first of the lyrics came as early as 1886. During the succeeding eight years the trickle was so slow that his great anxiety was lest it should altogether cease. Then came the flood of '95, and a ferment so terrific that the nervous reaction was well nigh insupportable, preyed on his mind so excessively that his dread of a recurrence forbade for years any further attempts, and to the end of life could only be recalled with torment.

He had written six of the poems before he set foot in Shropshire, but having decided on the title he felt he should pay the county a visit – 'to gain local colour', he added with a laugh and a look of derision.[1] The whole sixty-three lyrics of *A Shropshire Lad* were apparently composed during his afternoon walks. Either he memorized the lines, or occasionally made jottings on paper as he walked. In the former case, he had nothing to do on returning

[1] Through Mr. Laurence Housman I learn that the title was suggested by Dr. A. W. Pollard, when the complete MS. was submitted to him before publication. The statement in the text is precisely and unforgettably as A. E. H. made it to me.

home but to commit the afternoon's poem to paper, and possibly to make a few merely verbal emendations; in the latter, he filled in and completed at leisure. Sometimes the corrected drafts amounted to a dozen or more, sometimes to no more than two or three. When the process of gestation failed, the failure was invariably with the last verse, and safe deliverance would occasionally mean a three-weeks' struggle. This scrupulous care to effect his finished perfect ending, so consistently attained both in *A Shropshire Lad* and *Last Poems*, reminded me of the charge he had brought against Meredith's 'Love in the Valley' in Cambridge days, that it would have ended as well at any other as at its final verse.

He told me explicitly that four publishers[1] refused the MS. He gave the names, and among them I was troubled to hear that of my old friend A. H. Bullen. Strange that the scholar and connoisseur who discovered Campion, and delved to such purpose for other lost jewels of our English treasure, should also have done his best to exclude these newly-wrought additions to their number, on the only possible ground, one would suppose, that they were newly-wrought.

I tackled him seriously one day on two aspects of

[1] Many years later Housman casually referred to 'two or three' rejections, but certainly he told me four when the subject was first mentioned, and added the publishers' names.

a question that had long perplexed me: (1) the total indifference he appeared to show to the use of his verse for musical setting, and (2) that up to *The Chilswell Book* nothing of his was to be found in any anthology. He admitted the licence in the case of songs; it mattered nothing; words sung ceased to be poetry, and were not estimated as poetry. As for anthologists, he had given Bridges leave for obvious reasons, and lately he had given permission to Mr. Osbert Burdett, but had confined him to verses from *Last Poems*. The limitation in the latter case interested me. It confirmed my belief that his regard for *A Shropshire Lad* was like that of a mother for her first-born. Over and over again he showed a special, a tender, affection for it. He believed its lyrics were of higher quality than those of *Last Poems*. He was adamant against every proposition to bind the two volumes in one. He wished it presented and offered to the reader as a whole, and alone.

XIV

The last day of Housman's visits, certainly after the first one or two of them, showed him in a mood so strange, so poignant, and so baffling that a literal account of it must, I fear, incur a charge of exaggeration.

I choose one occasion of many, partly because of the exhibition it provides in contrasts, and partly because our younger daughter, who contributed so largely to the first phase overnight, shared with me the full discomfiture of the second, on the following afternoon. I had long before told her of the last hour experience of the visit, but all my talking had left her quite unprepared for the actuality.

Audrey had returned late on the Friday evening from her work in London. My wife, Housman and I had finished dinner, and were sitting as usual in the library, when she burst into the room, greeted Housman roundly, to which he responded with extreme cordiality, and a few minutes later departed to supper. When she returned to join us, I rather feared the first fine careless rapture might suffer reaction, and the promise excited by the greeting prove illusory. It did nothing of the kind. The result was the presentation of a Housman I had never before known, never suspected. Doubtless the girl's spirited and amusing talk and ready response played their part, but I felt no doubt the decisive ingredient was her complete freedom from self-consciousness and awe, the technique in short of perfect spontaneity. Within three minutes words were rattling to and fro, swift and keen and challenging, like the ball on a racquet court, and

70

the game never for a moment halted. Each com-
batant delivered, received, returned, manœuvred in
the spirit of sheer enjoyment. Yet the simile will
not serve. There could have been nothing more
remote from it than competitiveness; it was just a
joint display of wit, mirth and benevolence, in
which I occasionally chipped in; but in the main a
duet, in which Housman, drawing from his fund of
literary knowledge, played the bigger part, providing apt and unfamiliar illustrations, and furnishing forth many a merry tale. We all shared the
fun; I, I believe, monopolized the astonishment. It
was Audrey's first meeting with him.

The walk – our last walk – the following morning
passed as usual, the luncheon much as usual, and
then we all went into the library for coffee and for
Housman's last hour, my wife leaving us after a few
minutes. There he sat glum and tongue-tied. I
saw the consternation on Audrey's face, and how it
deepened when she found her efforts, some sparkling,
some provocative, all serious, all in vain. They were
addressed to him, but it was I responded, or, if
Housman, in the fewest, curtest words possible, like
the crack of a whip. I, too, played my part, and
questioned him, well knowing that nothing but
questions would serve to loosen those set lips, and
in the faint hope that some chance shot might be

71

effectual, perhaps soften the forbidding visage, and recover something of the spirit of the previous night. It was all in vain. Here was a lock to which there was no key.

The car was announced. In the hall he gave a curt good-bye to my wife and daughter. I walked with him down the flight of steps to the waiting car. He made not the smallest reference to the visit, repeated the same bare toneless almost impersonal good-bye, but as he grasped my hand, wordlessly, he turned on me the saddest and most haunting countenance I had ever seen on any face but his,

> . . . a look so piteous in purport
> As if it had been loosed out of hell
> To speak of —

I don't know what. The secret was his. I do know that on one especially of these several departures, I should have felt no surprise if he had bolted back to the house, and I had found him sitting stolidly in his accustomed chair.

X V

Once gone, and except for my customary yearly visit to Cambridge, there was not much to hope of intercourse until the next visit a year hence. For

Housman was not a letter-writer. The task, as I knew, came so hard to him that I made no attempt to impose it except at longish intervals. His own feelings on the question were expressed derisively, but I believe pretty literally as far as dislike went, in a letter that came in answer to a Christmas greeting, in which he said:

> It is true that I do not write to you, but then there are few people to whom I do, and never willingly. You write with ease, elegance, and evident enjoyment, whereas I hate it. Like Miss Squeers, I am screaming out loud all the time I write, which takes off my attention rather and I hope will excuse mistakes.

This was in the early years of our correspondence, and made the more graphic possibly to serve as a warning. Four years later he referred to the same subject in sardonic vein:

> If you wanted a letter at Christmas you did not go about the right way to get it, for you told me that my letter in the autumn was the only one I had ever written you, except in answer to one of your own; and this so filled me with consciousness of virtue, that I have been resting in contemplation of my merit ever since.

Our desultory correspondence continued at the rate of four or five yearly, to the end. His varied in quality, and much in length. A small number were the merest notes; to balance them an equal number perhaps running to six, or even eight, pages of ordinary writing-paper. Whatever the length, and whatever the quality, there was scarcely one that, had it come to me unsigned in the Great Sahara, I should not have greeted with confidence: 'Housman!' They were him as unquestionably as his talk, and had the same distinction, the same downrightness, economy, clarity, and never long absent a seasoning of mockery.

The letters that refer to visits filled the silences left by the spoken word: one in anticipation when he wrote:

> I shall be peculiarly grateful if I may pay you my visit some time in the week 15th-20th;

or in retrospect to my wife:

> I am home again from my delightful stay with you.

And when I wrote to tell him we were seriously contemplating departure from our home – the house he knew and the garden he so much liked – and moving to a humbler one, he replied:

> Whether you are in palace or cottage, I shall be very glad to come and see you in the summer.

He was always careful to give me information

about the Trinity dons I knew. If it were piquant, or his pen could give it a puckish touch, so much the more his enjoyment – and mine; and it might be he would slip in a comprehensive reference, as when he told me:

> Death and marriage are raging through the College with such fury that I ought to be grateful for having escaped both.

And again, on another subject of moment to Trinity,

> I am sorry it [the medicament I had recently started] has not yet brought you to the level of drinking audit ale, because this year's brew is quite good: last year's was a powerful explosive, and filled our cellars with the shards of bottles till we sent it back to its brewer, for use in case Yarmouth were bombarded again.

At the Christmas season there usually came a paean of praise and thanksgiving for the flesh-pots of Trinity, lavishly assembled to commemorate it – the side-table, the boar's head, and the rest. The jocular tone adopted did not, and clearly was not intended to, disguise the gusto with which he anticipated the good things, sought them, and demolished them. One December letter institutes a contrast, literally true I believe, and honest, though not greatly edifying, in which he would take a ghoulish pleasure. I had told him a few days previously of our plan to visit Germany and its picture galleries in the coming spring. He replied:

> I hope you will enjoy the weeks you mean to
> spend abroad, though I suppose that Burlington
> House at this moment [the Italian Exhibition]
> contains more of value than the galleries
> either of Dresden or Munich. Not that I
> should be able to tell. Stout and oysters are
> more on my level, and till midnight comes and ·
> brings them I can think of little else.

He tells me in December '26: 'My new edition of
Lucan sells just twice as fast as *A Shropshire Lad*
did'; and four years later: 'I have just finished the
last book I shall ever write, and now mean to do
nothing for ever and ever.'

XVI

Though far from wanting at any time, one
quality I delight to name was more evident in his
absence than in his presence. He assumed a shell of
callousness, and hid so well beneath it that one
might have met him long and familiarly in the
beaten path, and never suspected the disguise. His
chiselled speech, his stern and rather obdurate
physiognomy in respose, his sardonic quips, his
biting satire, his easy resort to mockery and scoffing:
of such was this outward vestment composed. And

it was a grim deceit. Underneath beat as warm and generous a heart, as willing for self-sacrifice, if the cause were true, as I have ever known. Not so instant in response perhaps — was there not that tegument to unbrace and cast off? — but sure and dogged and incommutable. In the beaten way of things he showed it, as I have already said, in his determined inquiries about one's health, or other source of trouble, and how earnestly he pursued the subject till he was satisfied of gaining the truth. He displayed the same concern over whatever I had mentioned as a cause of anxiety, remembered it, and recurred to the subject that had probably escaped my memory on his next visit. He did me more acts of kindness than I can number, services more valuable because only imaginative sympathy could have incited them, and determined purpose carried them through. Among many Cambridge friends it was he alone who thought of relieving my burden of homelessness, then in its fourth year, by introducing me to Mr. Jenkinson, University Librarian, and securing me the privilege of borrowing books at will, and also — a boon of almost daily utility — free use of the Union Buildings.

A service not easy to effect, and one that must have been intensely uncongenial, came in the weeks of the Coal Strike. I had chanced to tell him in a letter of the rather serious plight to which I personally should be exposed if the forecasts were realized. The Government official in control of the area in which we were situated happened to be dining in hall immediately after he received my letter. Housman laid the case before him, and was assured that should the difficulties arise I need but write to him and he would see they were removed. The need never arose, but an anxious fear was quieted.

His disclosures of the kind were few and exiguous, but they left no doubt of his constant benefactions in many directions and of many kinds. The off-hand way in which he referred to cases was but a disguise to kindnesses – some, as I know, of most generous extent – done in secret. Of these one can be told, for he told it to me in detail, and years later the sequel.

For many years he made holiday in Venice, and always employed the same gondolier, a man who proved much to his liking. News came one Christmas-time that he had developed tuberculosis, that he was laid aside, and that there was no hope of his ever returning to work. Mid-winter though it was, Housman straightway posted off to Venice, visited the gondolier in his home, and there had a legal document drawn up providing a sufficient income to secure the man's comfort so long as he lived. He ended his story by avowing that he should never go to Venice again.

The ill man lived on for many years, and while he lived Housman wrote to him, and in turn received reports of his condition, whether written by the patient or his priest, I do not remember. Housman told me when he died, and told me with considerable acerbity, how the relatives were pestering him to continue his gratuities, and copiously lying. The pleas were at first fawning, then suddenly passed to anger and vituperation. He too was angry, and I think very sore that a benefaction that had proved so useful to the recipient, so pleasant to himself to make, should end in mendacity and squabbling.

XVII

'Though I despise limited editions and will not let my publishers produce one, I did let the Riccardi Press do one of *A Shropshire Lad* in 1914.' This is the unpromising exordium of a reply to a request I made to him in the new year 1929. My friend F. L. M. Griggs R.A., had written to ask if I could persuade Housman to let Mr. Finberg print the two volumes of poems at his Alcuin Press in Chipping

Campden. I knew his contempt of all such things too well to bear the mission lightly, but Griggs was too dear a friend to disappoint merely on the chance of a refusal, phrased in terms however biting. Of a refusal I had little doubt. The subject had cropped up again and again in our talks, and always he had poured vials of scorn on what he called 'fine' printing, and emptied them to the last dregs on limited and autographed editions. The two requisites he asked of books, and the rest nothing, were that the type should be clear enough to read without effort, and the published price as small as practicable. We all know how scrupulously he carried the principle out in his own case, insisting, as he told me more than once, that when a reprinting was called for, *Last Poems* should follow the practice long in vogue with *A Shropshire Lad*, and, however diminutive its size or insignificant its appearance, be issued at as cheap a price as possible. He had no feeling whatsoever for printing or book production as a fine art, and I have heard him many times vigorously protest that his diminutive pocket editions at two shillings were good enough for anyone. There was something intensely piquant when, later, he vindicated his belief by giving our daughter the two volumes of this same edition, each with an inscription, as a wedding-present – probably as simple, and certainly as valued a gift as could have been given her.

I wrote, wrote with heavy misgivings, and impatiently awaited the verdict. It came, and was favourable. He resolutely refused to have the two volumes – *A Shropshire Lad* and *Last Poems* – bound as one, and he added peremptorily:

> I must warn you that I resist any alteration in the interest of what is supposed to be typographical beauty. I remember that the Riccardi Press transferred to the ends of lines dashes which I had put at the beginning, and I made them put them back. It is absolutely necessary that I should correct the proofs.

The first of these sentences and the last show his punctiliousness over punctuation, and of course spelling, but his total disregard, even contempt, for the lay-out of the printed page. The truth must be confessed that on the aesthetic plane, Housman, apart from his exquisite taste in poetry and the making of it, and his deep interest in and love of ecclesiastical architecture, stood a meagre and impoverished figure. He never began to feel, never suspected, that lettering could be a thing of beauty, or that type and spacing could as surely give delight to the eye as they could give offence. In our house almost every wall was hung with interesting watercolours: I never once saw him lift his face towards any of them. One wet afternoon he turned over my collection of Japanese colour-prints, and heaven knows what enjoyment he got out of the landscapes, certainly none out of the figures, whether by Harunobu, Kiyonaga, Shunman, or Utamaro. Of music he knew nothing, and confessed it meant nothing to him. I thought one evening in the library to quiet a reaction so tumultuous, following the gramophone records of Vaughan Williams' setting of four of his lyrics, that my wife, who sat near him, was momentarily expecting him to spring from his chair and rush headlong out of the room; and the torment was still on his suffused and angry visage when the records were finished, and I first realized the havoc my mistaken choice had caused. I thought to soothe him by playing some record of his own choosing. He looked rather lost when I asked him to name one, but presently suggested the Fifth Symphony, for the curious reason that he remembered to have heard it well spoken of. At the end he made a non-committal and quite colourless comment on the slow movement; the others he ignored. It was not the result one could have wished, nor did it suggest the desirability of continuing the music; for us at least it was enough that the turbulence was quieted and that we could now anticipate with confidence what remained of the evening's intercourse. Awhile back there seemed not the smallest prospect of an amiable issue; nor for a few moments could I conceive how to cope with the situation. It had arisen so unexpectedly, was so incomprehensible, and had gone to such excessive lengths. The astonishment was even greater than the disappointment. I had bought the Vaughan Williams records primarily in the hope of giving him pleasure, the intense pleasure, as I supposed, of hearing to what use a distinguished composer could put his verse.

It was the same, or much the same, with pictorial art. Year after year he had gone to Italy, the last many years to Venice, perhaps once or twice breaking the journey at Padua or Vicenza. I never once heard him mention Florence, its paintings, or its sculpture, though I believe he did pay it one visit; but never Ravenna, Perugia or Siena, the three Italian cities of which he said in a letter that people who found out he had never been to them 'always assure me they are the best in Italy'. Here is proof enough of his feeling for pictures. The riches of the *Trecento* and early *Quattrocento* were entirely lost on him. One day I suggested he might like to look at the exceedingly fine and detailed illustrations in Yashiro's book on Botticelli. He refused – and incidentally the refusal gave me the one and only opportunity I ever had of correcting him in error – on the ground that he cared nothing for paintings earlier than Giovanni Bellini. The two painters were of the same period.

Instead he turned to my half-dozen volumes of Max Beerbohm's Caricatures, and spent the entire afternoon with them in an easy chair by the window. I heard his repeated chuckles, and from time to time a burst outright of laughter. I believe he went through each volume twice, and many times I saw him return to a volume he had laid on one side, pick out the page he wanted, and chortle anew at the caricature it presented. He seemed – he was – thoroughly enjoying himself, and the spirit of cheerfulness was sustained at a higher level and for a longer period than at any time within my knowledge.

XVIII

One day in all the later visits, except the last, when Housman was too ill to go a whole day's outing, we spent among churches in the neighbouring counties of Northamptonshire and Gloucestershire. With a motor and a long summer's day at our disposal, no limit was set to the choice of itinerary;

we could go where we would, and by what route we would, guided solely by the desire to set out in high anticipation; and to return contented. I believe the purpose was realized, and now, remembered in tranquillity, motoring days count among the happiest and most prosperous that Housman spent with us. It was a sore disappointment, till familiarity blunted one's susceptibilities, that he so rarely expressed present enjoyment, or apparently wished himself suspected of it, and still more rarely, as though a thing taboo, any admission of past enjoyment. Indeed of this I do not recall a single instance in converse except his references to the companionship of A. C. Benson, a subject he always revived with glowing and undiminished zest. He could speak of Venice, of the Arena Chapel, of the Mantegna frescoes in the Eremitani, as non-committally as of an occurrence yesterday, to-day, or any day. The visible signs on our local pilgrimages together were little more conclusive. He generally wandered about the churches by himself, surveyed without comment, and, as I found many times later, remembered with astonishing retentiveness, for his visual memory was apparently no less reliable than his verbal. But – churches, all but one quite new to him, a landscape bathed in sunshine, the exhilaration of unfamiliar scenes, the Cotswold villages stone-walled, stone-roofed, lying in their folds of hill – all were things he cared greatly about: why wish acknowledgment? As it happened, on three occasions we got it unsought, three several occasions when he was surprised into expressions of astonishment, or of admiration and delight.

I took pains over all the itineraries. There was the not unimportant question of luncheon; indeed this was our only real difficulty, to find a hostelry convenient for our purpose, which was to inspect carefully chosen churches, and to ensure a decent meal. For the Cotswold country Cirencester and Stow-on-the-Wold were our halting places; the only inn we then knew in Northampton – and there was nothing but the town possible – was not seductive; but the fascination of the churches in the neighbourhood was so compelling, and I felt so satisfied of their rousing effect on Housman, whether of pleasure or of antiquarian astonishment only, that Northamptonshire was decided on as a first venture.

We began with Brixworth. It was farthest away, some ten miles beyond the county-town; it would allow of our visiting one of the two splendid churches in the town before lunch, and getting back not too late for tea – as long a day, we felt, as Housman might wish; while, between hope and dread, I was feverishly impatient to see how he would react to

Brixworth. A day or two previously he had amazed me by asking if there was any such thing as Saxon architecture, implying his total disbelief in its existence as a distinctive style. I had been reading and caring about Saxon architecture for thirty years and visited well over two hundred examples in different parts of the country, from Northumberland to the south coast, from Norfolk to Hereford, and never before realized that a shadow of doubt existed. Doubt was seventy years and more out of date, and to find it lingered on in a man like Housman was rather staggering. No wonder I was exercised in mind, apprehensive, and a little fearful. Here we were at the south door of Brixworth, the noblest, the most spacious, the best preserved of all Saxon churches: what would it do for him?

Once inside, it was startling to see his cynical bearing fall away, as palpably as if a physical gesture had removed an outworn garment. I did not think he was well pleased at being surprised into wonderment and admiration so unexpected, and perhaps still less to behold at a glance, wherever his eyes rested, the compelling proof of Saxon architecture, or at any rate of a style and a craftsmanship the like of which in all his church visiting he had never before seen. Our customary relations were reversed: here was something about which he knew nothing;

I talked, he listened, and though I noticed he asked no questions, he complacently accepted a position to which he must have been singularly unaccustomed — *in statu pupillari* — and at first it appeared not too willingly.

We lingered a long time at the church, both inside and out, restoring its original plan, its missing portions, grappling with its fascinating problems; discussing its crudities of masonry, so anomalous in a building of such grandiose scale — a scale so ambitious that it is tempting to suppose the tempestuous Wilfrid of Hexham must have been the moving spirit — and finding, in short, nothing too trivial to pass over. If I continued to expound, it was that Housman soon forgot our novel relationship, grew more and more interested, and more responsive, and was to all appearance wholly content, not least, I fancied, with the reconstruction of the seventh-century building, and its many insoluble puzzles.

We returned at length to Northampton, but before going to lunch we decided to inspect Holy Sepulchre, the second in date of the four round churches still surviving in England — and so much else, its spacious additions, which in conjunction with the original round church, displayed all the styles of medieval architecture from 1100 to *c*. 1400, in unbroken sequence. Here again I had the high satisfaction of telling Housman many things he could not discern, however well versed, on a casual visit, and of straightening out the complexities arising from the extensive changes that had occurred in the process of three centuries' growth; and again he showed the keenest interest and enjoyment. He was now on familiar ground and could set in order and assess, with a little help, all he looked on, and so for him the prosperous morning ended, as sight-seeing should, on its topmost note.

Wherever possible I like to win a crescendo effect, and I felt the surest confidence the afternoon visit would accomplish it. Housman, I found, had never heard of St. Peter's, Northampton, and therefore was utterly unprepared for anything so unique, so rich, so uniform, so beautiful. Never before or since have I seen him so taken aback, or his frozen restraint so completely melted. For once, and this once only, he burst into exclamation. His face glowed with astonishment and pleasure. He was momentarily transformed, back, as I could not but feel, to some state of long ago – his hidden self freed and a sudden and surprised delight had effected the transformation.

XIX

I believe he thoroughly enjoyed all the days we spent among churches, though as time went on he became rather scornful of what he guessed to be my predilection for those of Saxon and Norman date. If meant as a reproach to my pilotage it was undeserved, for I chose only those I knew to be rewarding, regardless of style and period, and they included examples of all periods, like the refined and graceful Early English work at Warmington (Northants), the grandiloquent sixteenth-century Cirencester, and several where he got the reticulated windows and flowing curvilinear tracery to which he was peculiarly partial. But it so happens that most of the fascinating churches of both Northamptonshire and Gloucestershire are of the two earliest periods. And what more intriguing than the two Norman doorways of Quenington, or the delicious Norman chancel at Elkstone, or the charming simplicity of Daglingworth, Coln Roger, and Duntisbourne Rouse, or the massive grandeur of Langford? To all which, I believe, he succumbed.

But the only later visit that at all compared in spectacular impressiveness with that first one was the one we spent at Tewkesbury and Deerhurst. I do not remember whether he had seen Tewkesbury before. I believe not. Nor do I remember that he made any comments – probably none; or showed more than a passive demeanour; for it was easily possible for Housman to wander about even so glorious a fane as Tewkesbury, even on a first visit, without displaying the smallest indication of what he was feeling, unless it were by his willingness to prolong his wandering.

Moreover, he was not in a yielding mood on that particular day, rather was it a forbidding mood, as was evident not only from his clouded look, but from an occurrence in the earlier part of the journey. I had broken a long silence by calling out to him to look at the willow-herb. At that moment it could be seen – a ravishing sight – stretching in endless profusion along a steep declivity below the lane. In another moment it would be too late. 'Look at the willow-herb!' I called. 'It isn't willow-herb,' he snapped back angrily, 'it's rose-bay.' I should have thought the generic name had been good enough, but at all times he was nothing if not exact, and in that mood contumelious.

Deerhurst restored him to amiability. As we approached the church from the south side there was nothing to awaken curiosity save the gawky Saxon tower, markedly oblong in shape, and slightly battering as it rises. All else presented to view was the ugly shell, added many centuries later, enclosing the south aisle, enclosing too the precious tenth-century core. The liveliest interest is quickened the moment you enter the west door, in the disposition of the walled spaces at the base of the tower, and not even Brixworth has so many thrilling features, or such unique openings, with their massive triangular heads and fluted pilasters, as the west wall of the Deerhurst nave. And there is lots besides: a clearly discernible ground-plan, showing side-chambers or primitive transepts on either side the nave, and an apse at the east end; a lofty chancel arch, moulded, and springing from capitals of unique and puzzling design; the mysterious chambers in the tower, and their still more mysterious openings, east and west; a contemporary font unmatched for the richness, intricacy and beauty of its carving; and away at the eastern exterior, rewarding vigilance, a winged angel, recalling the Spinello Aretino at Arezzo, on a slab set in a triangular recess.

We surveyed the church pretty thoroughly. It is the relic of Saxon England that has given me intenser pleasure, and more engrossed me, than any other. How I could bear to show its ravishments to an apathetic onlooker, or what the consequences, I don't know. Fortunately the visit did not put endurance to the test. Housman was quite certainly interested, responsive and inquiring, not exuberantly as I could have wished, but appeasingly.

After lunch in Tewkesbury, we wandered over the meadows, at his express wish, to see the water-meet between Avon and Severn. It provided an unfortunate contretemps. After an hour's wandering over dense tangled grass, and all of us rather wearied, we decided to return. Housman was positive of the direction; both my wife and I believed him mistaken. This angered him, and we yielded – to find, after long floundering over hummocky ground, that the river we were following – whether Avon or Severn, I do not remember – was the wrong one, and was diverting us farther and farther from the town. A chance native set us right. The rest was silence – and fatigue.

Before leaving home in the morning, my wife had telephoned to Lady Wemyss to ask if we might call for tea on the return journey. Stanway lay directly on our route, it was always for us a most delectable house of call, and I knew the pleasure it would give Lady Wemyss to see Housman, and him to see her and her beautiful Jacobean home. They had met at our house the previous year, along with

93

the present Poet Laureate and Mrs. Masefield, and we did not forget that, whatever the conviviality attained that day, it was due to Lady Wemyss, to her vivacity, her infinite skill in putting strangers at their ease with herself and one another, her naïve and winning spontaneity, and her own animated and abounding talk in endless variety.

We found several guests there, all relatives, and all charmingly friendly. Tea was served in the great hall, soaring to its timbered roof, with an open fireplace midway on one side, and on the other – a feature that caught one's breath anew on every visit – an immense oriel window, towering from floor to ceiling in tier upon tier of slender lights, filled to thrilling effect with the green humpy glass that must have been contemporary with the house. While conversation was being promiscuously bandied about, I noticed how ill at ease Housman looked; a deep flush was on his face, to the roots of his hair; he did not volunteer, as far as I could see, a single remark; spoke only when spoken to; and before tea was over, the efforts of those near him entirely ceased. At this stage our hostess came to the rescue, and carried him off to see the house, its beautiful façade, its famous many-roomed gateway, and the bewitching composition it made with the tiny stone-walled, stone-roofed hamlet and church, all grouped harmoniously at the foot of a lengthy slope of wooded hill.

I was credulous enough to suppose, once we had started on our homeward journey, that the one inevitable consequence of our call at Stanway must be a spontaneous disclosure, however fragmentary and non-committal, of Housman's impressions. The house was new to him, and probably no more beautiful Jacobean house, more perfectly situated, or more picturesque in its surroundings of climbing woodland and stone-roofed hamlet, could be found anywhere. Enough, I thought, to fill the whole hour's run home with talk, and if the subject wore thin, then the morning's plenty to hark back to. We were soon mounting Stanway hill, with its wide and lovely outlook over the valley, and there in the distance lay Bredon, prominent as though in greeting to the poet who had brought her world-wide fame. And still the silence was unbroken. My wife and I, carefully avoiding any mention of our call – that, we felt, was Housman's prerogative – exchanged a casual remark on the passing scene, no more . . . a whole hour, the crowded acquisitions of the day, and not a word from Housman, either of reminiscence or comment.

Housman was accustomed to salt his talk with phrases sometimes arresting by their exquisite precision and shapeliness, sometimes and more rarely by their withering content. When he meant venom, venom it was, stark and undisguised; and it could be counted on inevitably when the few subjects of his special aversion came under review. Of these, the two I found most unfailing were a distinguished novelist and playwright – but why, I could never surmise, and never sought to know, but a virulent manifestation of which a brief account will be given directly; and women. Housman was an avowed misogynist, and so faithful to his vow that he affirmed it more distantly in demeanour, pungently in words, on all occasions. His feelings appeared to possess the inevitability of instinct. He was painfully ill at ease in the company of women, flushed and distraught, as in the instance I have just given, or positively rude, and intentionally rude, in phrase and manner, as on the occasion mentioned towards the end of these memories.

I remember his telling me of a Cambridge hostess who had greatly attracted him. He had been to her house several times with increasing enjoyment, and had begun to build on the acquaintance as a surety of pleasures to come. Then followed a swift reverse. On a later visit, he added with a darkened countenance and bitter tongue, he had come to the conclusion that the lady's purpose was simply to run him as a lion. This determined, her charm and the seductions of her hospitality went for nothing. 'This must cease!' he said angrily as the recital came to end, 'she has seen the last of me'; and straightway the attractive hostess had fallen from her temporarily exalted position to the status he ascribed to women in general. With my wife he was amiability itself. She never fussed, never bothered him, either with adulation or perfunctory talk; and because of their perfectly natural relations, I well knew the last obstacle to his visits was removed.

I never attempted to commit any of his epigrammatic sayings to paper. There was no opportunity at the moment of delivery, and only a vastly more retentive memory than mine could have preserved till later the verbal exactitude so necessary for effective repetition. But certain of his comments and opinions I did note down, I fear very haphazardly; and a brief selection of them, along with a few excerpts from letters, may, I think, be of sufficient interest to quote. Various as their topics are, I find it convenient to give them here in sequence.

Dr. Johnson did not possess poetic sensibility. As for the *Lives of the Poets*, there were few of them worth writing, and they never would have been written at any other period.

I always keep Selden's *Table-Talk* at hand, often turn to it, and always find it serviceable and cleansing. When engaged in writing I have made constant use of it as a corrective both of slip-shod and flummery, as a guide to follow as faithfully as can be.

My lectures are no trouble to me, but I find I cannot get up a real interest in work and study. I read chiefly novels and Lecky's History of England in the eighteenth century, from which I learn much which I did not know (November 1933).

Could you believe it? At an early period of manhood I memorized cricket averages, and could reel them off correctly to two decimal points.

I too am pleased with the noise about *The Testament of Beauty*, excessive though it is. He himself [Bridges] rates it at its true value and calls it this blatant and incontinent boom.

I think Masefield is the right Laureate. Newbolt, who would do the job best, is too little of a poet.

I can truthfully say that I hate and despise money. [What occasioned the confession I do not remember. It came during one of our morning walks, and made a deep impression on me because of the tremendous emphasis with which it was spoken – an emphasis more demonstrative than he indulged at any other time.]

The greatest blessing and the one undiluted bounty of this life is a sudden and painless end. My *Ultima Thule* is the death that Bevan [Reader in Arabic at Cambridge] died – dinner in Hall among his friends as usual, the customary evening walk, the accustomed rest on one of the seats on the Backs, and – an end.

The remaining incidents I give in my own words:–

In a moment of jocularity, after quizzing Housman on the subject of the honorary degrees I had been told on unimpeachable authority he had refused from at least seven Universities, I asked if it were true he had also refused the Order of Merit. 'Ah!' he laughed, 'wouldn't you like to know?' I had never thought to extract more than a niggardly 'yes' or 'no', and I felt satisfied I had achieved it.

He constantly referred to the novels of Arnold Bennett, and always in terms of warmest admiration. Of *The Old Wives' Tale* he spoke on many occasions with an enthusiasm rare in him at all times and on any subject.

His attitude towards another contemporary writer – John Galsworthy – was singular and was inexplicable. It revealed a violent personal antipathy. So much so, that, on the first mention of Galsworthy's name, the animus was so pronounced I felt it was a subject scrupulously to avoid for the future. The bitterness of feeling was shown when, years later, Housman made his last mention of Galsworthy. He told me how proudly he had accepted the office of pallbearer at the funeral of Thomas Hardy in Westminster Abbey. The following day he saw in the press that Galsworthy was to be one of the number, wrote immediately to decline the office, and only capitulated as a consequence of Barrie's entreaties.

XXI

The briefest of his visits to us after the first hasty one was in 1933. It had been long arranged that he was to come as usual for the customary five days, but as the date drew near he wrote from a Nursing Home in Cambridge to tell me that he had been confined to the Home ever since the Senate House lecture on 'The Name and Nature of Poetry', and that he was still there under strict medical surveillance, and that there was no possibility of his coming to us. A week later came a second letter to say that he was back again in his rooms, and must go in a few days to see his widowed sister-in-law in Worcestershire, and might he come to us for lunch en route.

He arrived by car a little while before the meal was due, following his regular practice of recent years of motoring from Bletchley. A first glimpse showed how greatly he was changed in appearance. He looked strangely worn and frail, so much more than could have been expected from a comparatively brief confinement to bed, imposed solely for the purpose, as he had assured me, of rest and medical supervision. It was gladdening and a good deal of a relief to my anxiety, when, on seeing the variety of wines awaiting his choice, he broke into a chortle so hearty, so like the amused gratification of old times, that I could not but suspect my apprehensions were largely groundless.

The meal over, we strolled at his wish about the garden. It was a very beautiful day – June at its loveliest, a cloudless sky overhead, but the heat tempered by a delicious breeze. We had reached the long border when he suddenly stopped, faced me, and asked abruptly: 'Were you surprised at not receiving a copy of my lecture?' 'Yes,' I replied, 'so surprised that I delayed ordering it for several days after publication, in the sure belief that you would be sending me one.' In the pause that followed he showed no inclination to renew the walk, but still stood fixed, still facing me, and looking inexpressibly wistful and sad. I couldn't conceive what was coming. Then, after what seemed a long and crowded silence, and speaking with extreme vehemence, he went on: 'Well, you didn't get one because I haven't given a copy to anyone. I take no pride in it. I would rather forget it, and have my friends forget. I don't wish it to be associated with me.'

Then, as we began pacing backwards and forwards again, he launched on the whole story of the lecture, from its inception to its delivery, speaking now with greater deliberation, but with sustained emphasis to the end.

He said he ought never to have undertaken the office, and he knew it. But he felt the invitation a great honour, and it was conveyed in such flattering terms by Professor Trevelyan that he couldn't see any justification for refusal; and succumbed.

From that hour his days had been an unabated torment. He had awakened every morning to the dread of a task to which he could bring no heart, and a struggle that had never given him a moment's satisfaction, or could give. No man, he said with pained conviction, could possibly achieve anything worth while under such conditions. The actual delivery of the lecture had caused him no trouble, even he had enjoyed it, and his face brightened as he made the admission – which meant no more, I suppose, than that the excitement of declaiming before a distinguished and highly appreciative audience had coruscated away all memories of the toil he had endured and his grim dissatisfaction with the result.

The recital had occupied some five to ten minutes. He had talked with few and momentary pauses, and with such an urge of feeling that I greatly feared the consequences in a man advanced in years who had so recently risen from a bed of sickness and was obviously still so far from well. Garden chairs were at hand, and I had long been waiting an opportunity to propose we should go to them, and be seated. But the opportunity had never come. He was too intent on the subject to be interrupted, and the pacing to and fro along the border was done with the same settled determination, as though if the one were stopped the other must stop.

The end came voluntarily, and I begged him to sit down and rest. He looked flushed and a good deal spent, but he assured me he was all right, and certainly the strained expression of countenance had gone, and was replaced by one of relief, ease, and satisfaction. My wife joined us, he talked cheerfully, and a while later took his leave.

Later in the summer he went a motor tour in France, accompanied by a French friend. I believe Touraine. It was a failure. On his return he wrote:

> I am sorry to say that after my holiday I am worse rather than better. In previous visitations of this nervous trouble I have been physically strong and able to take good long walks; but at present, though my heart appears to be all right again, I am feeble.

XXII

The letters of the last three years tell of a steady decline in health. The first note of foreboding had been struck in a letter of May 1933, when he wrote: 'I have grown older in the last twelvemonth.' That was the year of the lecture, and the ominous year in which the promised visit was prevented by his detention in the Nursing Home.

The following year he came as usual, came for the whole inside of a week in mid-June. Health and vigour appeared to be little changed from aforetime. We went our customary walks, and spent one of the days among churches. I did not then realize it, but the visit was the last paid to our Souldern home, and to the garden he found so much enjoyment in.

It was a visit that stands apart from all others; and looking backward I find that memory most readily recovers the incidents associated with it, and lingers over them most wistfully. They included the evening our daughter returned from London and transfigured Housman to volubility and mirth, and the unique event of a walk in which he, not I, did all the talking. But there was something else, and something much more treasurable than these. These were incidental; what was fundamental and new and precious was the clearer emergence of Housman himself, the glimpses he allowed me into his buried life, the touch of intimacy.

The following May, in anticipation of his visit, he wrote: 'I fear I shall not be a worthy walking-companion for you.' No more, but it was a note of foreboding for which I was totally unprepared. Only the year before we had gone our usual four- or five-mile walks, and he had seemed to enjoy them as usual, and showed no signs of fatigue. He added the grim comment, apropos the experience of a common friend: 'One advantage of living in this charming world is that however bad one may think one's own lot it is always easy to find someone whose lot is worse.'

Unquestionable as the foreboding was it did not appear to prognosticate immediate danger, or anything more than the decline in strength to be expected at the age of seventy-five. Wherefore it came as a shock, when, six weeks later, and a few days before his visit was due, he wrote to postpone it, wrote in pencil from the Nursing Home, and for the first time revealed the nature of his illness and the symptom indicative of its very advanced stage:

> You probably know all about Cheyne-Stokes breathing described in Arnold Bennet's [*sic*] Clayhanger: sleepless nights spent in recurrent paroxysms of failure of breath, which can be combated if one is broad awake, but which overwhelm one if one dozes . . . If I were in proper health I should at this moment be representing Cambridge at the tercentenary of the French Academy.

This seemed the final doom to all my delighted anticipation of introducing him to our new home. I could not believe it possible that, even though his condition improved, he would feel well enough to face the journey, or could feel sufficient inducement to brave the inconveniences and risks. An exchange of letters showed that the only doubt in his mind

was whether we could conveniently keep an uncertain date open for him. We could indeed. We
did; and ten days later he came.

XXIII

I felt it probable he might resent, seriously ill
as he had been, any suggestions for relieving the
discomforts of a tedious journey, such as it had been,
by train to Bletchley, and on by car. I dreaded the
thought of his having to endure, only two days
after leaving the Home, any unnecessary hardships;
and after much deliberation and many qualms I
wrote to ask if he would be willing for me to go to
fetch him; and waited. Not even the monitory
name 'Cheyne-Stokes' conveyed so vivid an impression of his state as the readiness with which he
consented.

We halted on the way home at Buckingham. Tea
refreshed him, but both before and after he talked
little, and I knew he wished for silence. After the
customary exchanges after a year's separation, I
believe his only spontaneous remark was to tell me
he had brought me a copy of his *Three Poems: The
Parallelogram, The Amphisbaena, The Crocodile,*
privately printed at University College, London.

He added: 'You won't think much of them because I don't myself.' He thought of them well enough to write my name in the book the following morning, and I thought well enough of the possession to add it to my inscribed copies with highest relish.

An hour after our arrival the President of Magdalen and Mrs. Gordon came for the night. It was a long standing engagement in renewal of former meetings, and far too rich in promise to relinquish unless Housman should feel the strain too great on his first evening. I had written to put the facts before him, and begged him to decide solely on personal grounds: Mrs. Gordon would perfectly understand if they had to be put off. No, certainly they must come, he replied: he would be delighted to see them.

That evening is ever-memorable, but nothing of it so memorable as Housman's vitality, high spirits, and good companionship. Against such a background as I have recorded, the memory seems sheer phantasy. How, after his recent grave condition, and with a heart in the critical state it was in, how it was possible that he should show not the smallest indication of ill-health, or physical disability, but on the contrary talk abundantly and well, and laugh and keep us in laughter with a flow of excellent stories, I cannot conceive. The best in everyone is,

I should suppose, the customary attendant on the presence of the President of Magdalen, and to him, I feel, the success of that evening was mainly due; but that Housman should, in his state of health, have been capable of his best, and given it with so much exuberance, spontaneity and obvious enjoyment, seemed to me, who knew the facts, simply incredible.

And it proved equally incredible to the Gordons when I told them the following morning how serious Housman's condition had been, and still was. They were lost in amazement.

XXIV

In every subsequent hour of the visit my wife and I were given only too painful evidence of the true state of affairs. Housman had become suddenly old and broken. We gave our pleasant sitting-room – the one sitting-room in the old portion of the house – up to him. It was far from all disturbing sounds and movements; it was refreshingly cool even in a season of excessive heat; and there, sitting by an open window, he spent the whole day from breakfast to dinner dozing or cursorily turning over newspapers and old magazines, and reading betimes a book he had brought with him, but what it was I never inquired, lest curiosity ever so innocent should worry him. It was peace he wanted, and he looked the embodiment of peace. My wife and I went in to him at long intervals to avoid all appearance of neglect, and to tend any want. If there was aught more than a sad grateful acknowledgment, and perhaps a smile, or sometimes an unrelieved gloom, it was to ask for a fresh supply of the home-made iced lemonade, which, at my wife's suggestion, he usually kept beside him.

He spent the entire morning and afternoon indoors, but after tea each day he proposed a walk. Before he came I had carefully decided the routes he might safely be taken in order to avoid rough ground and all but the gentlest gradients. We kept punctiliously to the ordained course the first two evenings; on the third he insisted on climbing to the top of one of a group of little hills clustered round us. I felt it was unwise, felt it was running a grave risk even; but we went, leisurely and with many pauses. He appeared none the worse, and my anxious watch discovered no trace of ill. It was on the summit that he made his one and only comment on a countryside he had never before seen. It was a mere ejaculation, and it was favourable.

But of our new home, its garden, its stream, its

situation, no mention passed his lips. Nor did he
from first to last make the least reference or inquiry
about the trials we had endured, the extensive
alterations we had made in converting an ancient
water-mill to modern needs and comforts, or how
far we were satisfied with the result. It was
characteristic, as I have before said, but a characteristic exercised in this instance of all others could
only be explained, I felt sure, on grounds of health.
The unquestioning and the silence were not as in
former days. They seemed indicative of a mind
remote from transitory things. He was more ill,
and felt more ill, than we knew, and his quiet and
disinterestedness were the signs. After dinner he
brightened; the rest of the day he wished only for
peace, wished to be left alone, effortless and undis-
tracted, with his own burdened thoughts.

He looked ill and sad and anguished the first
morning, a consequence, I felt probable, due largely
to his journey the previous day and to the excessive
animation he had shown throughout the evening.
He had had one of his bad nights – the sort of night
and its miseries he had often told me about; that he
dreaded, and found well nigh intolerable; that
seemed unending, and made ruin of many hours
of the following day. He had experienced these
visitations at intervals, and spoken of them, since his

first visit to the Nursing Home three years ago; of late they had been more devastating, more frequent, and night-long. It was because he felt incapable of combating them any longer alone and unaided that he had paid his recent visit to the Home.

Such a night was the last, and while he talked of it, it occurred to me that he might be glad to have his morning tea brought earlier – the earlier the sooner his relief, for he had told me how impatiently he awaited it, and how it revived him. He looked all wonderment and eagerness when the suggestion was made, but was it practicable? – how could it be done? I replied, nothing easier; that I was up at six, or soon after, boiled my kettle, and was back in bed with books and tea some ten minutes later, and could undertake to have a cup at his bedside at latest by 6.30, if that would suit him.

And it was done. Each morning I knocked on his door at the appointed moment, and always he was propped up in bed, reading. The whole weight of illness and dolour was on his face. I longed to arrange his pillows: had they been in the service of an anchorite of the desert they could hardly have afforded less comfort. But it was an occasion for dispatch. A word of greeting from me, a doubtful response, if any, from him, the cup deposited on the table by his side, and I was gone. I knew there was a conflict between gratitude and rebelliousness going on, and pityingly I left him alone with it.

After breakfast he retired to his cool and quiet corner in the sitting-room, and returned to it, as though obedient to a compelling need, directly luncheon was over. If the garden called him, he seemed to pay no heed to the call. The window where he sat so many hours of the day looked out upon the pleasantest of scenes – a wide lawn, a flower border, a selvedge of scrub, and beyond it fields sloping gently upward to a long line of hill; but his low chair was so placed that he could see no more at best than a broken fragment of the picture, nothing of the garden, only the distant contour of hill. Either, as I have told, he was holding a book uncomfortably at arms' length, or delving promiscuously in newspapers and magazines that lay on the table before him, or, more often than not, sleeping, sometimes so soundly that a quiet entry did not waken him.

I found it a sad and moving spectacle. To leave him so much to himself, passing the time, it seemed, so ineffectually, and so at the mercy, one could not but fear, of disquieting thoughts, was not easy; it was indeed a perpetual source of discomfort and self-reproach. Yet it was clearly what he most wished. Of that my wife was more convinced than I. Where

I saw only neglect, desuetude and loneliness, she
saw contentment and tranquillity. But it was a
word from Housman himself that set my mind at
rest. I had gone into the room on one of the four
or five brief visits I paid during the day, when he
laid his book down, and, with a surge of feeling
that seemed on the very verge of tears, he spoke
of the delicious quiet of the room – he had rarely
experienced such stillness, such undisturbed peace,
anywhere, at any time – and what it had meant to
him, and how grateful he felt for it. I do not give
the exact phrases he used. His words were few,
and deeply impressive, yet the look on his face told
even more than they.

It was just what I most longed to hear. I had
never thought to have my doubts and fear so comfortably allayed. But for a confirmation in writing
two days after he had left us – left us for the last
time – I could well believe that desire, and not
actuality, had shaped the memory, and coloured it.
He wrote to my wife:

> I was glad to hear that you said I seemed
> happy while with you, for indeed the fact was
> so, and everything conspired to give me peace
> and enjoyment, and I make warm return of
> thanks to you and your husband for your care
> and kindness.

XXV

Considering his recent illness and its grave import, it is almost incredible that, later in the summer, a few weeks after he had left us in a still precarious state of health, he should have carried out his original design of a motor tour in Dauphiné and Savoy. He was accompanied by a French acquaintance with whom he had never travelled before, and of whose solicitude and care he wrote most warmly when the holiday was over. In a lengthy letter, written a few days after his return, he spoke of the 'pleasant' tour, of the scenery being more magnificent than he had guessed, of the engineering of the roads rivalling the works of God, of the many good restaurants, and their excellent Rhone wines. And then he recounted an incident that might well have had disastrous consequences. They were setting off from Lyons on the first day of the tour, when, as he stepped into the car, he banged his head so violently that he had to be taken to a hospital. There the scalp wound he had sustained was stitched and bandaged – so well done, he added, and so quickly has it healed that the doctors exclaim at it.

It did not interfere with my movements, and I continued in the same taxi the outing I had planned for the day.

He returned to England by air. It was a disagreeable journey in consequence of stormy weather, which was unpropitious enough to cause a three hours' wait 'before the aeroplane could pluck up courage to start'.

He could afford to speak slightingly of the aeroplane's craven-heartedness when he himself was just returning from a tour that had exhibited so signal a display of courage and endurance – for an ill man, at the age of seventy-five, a fortitude truly heroic. For he well knew the risks he was running daily of prolonged illness and perhaps death in a foreign land, or, the least of them, the possibility of finding that he was after all unequal to the effort, and the consequent disappointment to himself and his companion. Apparently the only misadventure was the scalp injury, and it says much for his strength of constitution that it occasioned so little inconvenience. He enjoyed the holiday in his cool and calculating way, and he believed he was the better for it.

But the beneficial effects were of short duration. In a letter dated December 1, he wrote:

When I came back from France I was in fair

fettle, perhaps due to living in motor cars and hotels and always using lifts; but I soon began to go rapidly down hill, so that I had to abandon my old rooms, where the 44 stairs were too much for me.

I decided I must go the first possible day to see him. There seemed no reason he should know — rather the reverse — that I proposed a visit to Cambridge solely for the purpose. My letter merely said that I should be there on the date named, and would be glad if he could see me for half an hour after tea. I hoped the choice of hour, whether he should be dining in hall or in his own room, would show that I was not looking to him for hospitality. My last wish was to tax his strength, or to disturb in the least his invalid habits.

His reply was a cordial welcome for the visit and the hour I had suggested, but also it invited me peremptorily to dinner unless I were already engaged.

Dinner was in the new Combination Room, the Vice-Master at the head of the table, and not more than ten dons present. We remained for the wine to complete its immemorial three circuits, after which I returned with Housman to his room for about an hour. In the hour I had spent with him before dinner he had shown me round the whole of his new suite. It was good to find him so charmingly situated, and so undisguisedly proud and appreciative of the conveniences and comforts, even, I thought, of the almost feminine graciousness. Instead of the chilling dreary quarters in Whewell's Court, and the forty-odd stone steps to reach them, he was now on the ground floor, and had for every exit and entrance, the spacious and unwearying greeting of the Great Court, and indoors everything he could desire for personal satisfaction. His only fear, he said, was lest the profusion of foliage round the windows in summer should obscure the view and darken the room — a fear he never lived to prove or disprove.

Ill as he was, and under obvious physical duress, his wonted fire of despite flared up while he recounted, without a word, his or mine, to suggest the subject, the satisfaction he had found in destroying a portrait of himself that had hung, I know not how long, in the Combination Room at Trinity. I knew his excessive dislike of the drawing, not as a work of art, but as being what he considered a libellous representation, and his annoyance at seeing it exalted in a situation that seemed to avouch its truthfulness as a likeness, and that must convey this belief to posterity, not Trinity's alone. Previous references to the portrait had both surprised and amused me; they cropped up, as on this occasion, apropos of nothing; they showed a resentment always ready to break into flame; and, knowing the drawing familiarly, and, finding it perfectly recognizable, I could not but attribute the feeling displayed to a quite unexpected trait of personal vanity. I was forcibly reminded of the contrast with Robert Bridges. One summer afternoon, in his library at Chilswell, the magnificent old man took me through a portfolio of his portraits, all signed by familiar names – drawings in various media, etchings, and photographs of oil paintings. He chortled gleefully as he passed one after another on to me; guffaw followed guffaw; and as they drew to an end, 'each worse than the last', he exclaimed laughingly, and bundled them back irreverently into their case. The wholesomeness and sufficiency of mirth could hardly have been more effectively displayed – not a touch of malice or umbrage, few words, a quizzing question or two, a good-humoured comment, whether of disparagement or qualified approval, a continual ripple of laughter, in which I felt it good to share, though by no means always approving the Poet Laureate's judgment, but of that judgment there could be no doubt whatsoever, and it was not favourable.

How Trinity ever came to possess the drawing of

Housman, he did not tell me, nor did I inquire. At all times I was chary of evincing curiosity in his personal affairs, or of risking questions that might prove disquieting, and particularly when, as on the present occasion, the flushed face, hurried staccato speech, and strained look were a deterrent, for me at least, to aught but silence or acquiescence. As the story unfolded I found his excitation was but in part due to retailing the retrospective grievance; he was angry at the price exacted for its relief. Trinity had relinquished its portrait on the sole condition that Housman replaced it with one in his own possession, by the same artist. And this one also he had destined for the same fate. I might judge, he said with a curl of lip, and look crowded with venom – I might judge his opinion of the first drawing by the fact that he was willing to purchase its removal by substituting one he had never intended should survive him, least of all on a wall of Trinity College.

The tirade ended swiftly as it had begun, and after a brief breathing space he suggested a personally conducted tour. He showed his bath-room with the nearest approach to enthusiasm, almost adolescent glee, I had ever known him display. He pointed out the various fittings that nothing should escape me. There was boiling water at every hour of the twenty-four. It was this provision that had been his great surprise, as it was the blessing he most prized. Did I know how it was effected? I did, for it happened to be the device installed at home; but I feigned astonishment, so much was he relishing his novel office of showman. It was good to see him so well furnished with homely comforts, and to know the satisfaction they gave him; but all the while I was silently regretting they had come about when so little time was given him to enjoy, and when already he was too infirm and broken to reap their fullest benefits. And I was thinking that here, as in even greater deprivations, the responsibility lay at his own door. There must have been numberless opportunities of escape from the dreariness and discomforts of Whewell's Court, and from, for him, the serious exaction of a steep flight of forty-four steps every time he went abroad. The most recent chance befell, as he had described to me graphically at the time, some three years previously. He was then persuaded to go to a suite of rooms in the gatehouse. All was ready for occupation. A lift had been installed, I believe entirely at his own expense. At the eleventh hour he recanted; he had rather sacrifice the immense gain in charm and ease of situation, in comparative freedom from undergraduate clamour, and in escaping the toilsome climb, than face the few hours' upheaval, or per-haps, to his sensitive spirit, the more formidable dread of relinquishing quarters that had long been home to him, and the scene of many of his most famous achievements in scholarship. Such in-fluences would weigh decisively with Housman, and when at last they were out-weighed, I suspect it was entirely due to medical representations. I did not question him on the subject. He was so well contented with the move, now it had taken place, so enthusiastic about its benefits, that I feared the possibility of recalling any struggles and contentions that were passed.

At the night visit I kept strictly to the hour's duration. He seemed to enjoy the desultory chat, though he talked little. But for my knowledge of his condition medically, he looked so well that I should never have supposed he was in other than normal health. He preserved his erect well-knit figure, his bright complexion, at all times a con-spicuous feature, and now perhaps emphasized by the black skull-cap he was wearing as a protection to the scar left by the accident in Lyons, his resonant voice, and his clear incisive utterance. He was to all appearance so much the Housman I had first known, that it seemed impossible to believe that he was old, as years go, and his life precarious, and that in all human probability, when I came to say good-bye, it would be for the last time.

As I sat watching him my thoughts ran swiftly over the past, more haltingly towards the future. I remembered my good fortune in having won a larger share of Housman's favours than fell to most of his acquaintances, and for once, I think, my pride and thankfulness were not impaired by the wonderment that usually accompanied the reflection: how possibly I could have achieved the privilege in such unaccustomed measure. Then to the future, and what his death would mean to me – an end of my yearly memorable visits to him at Trinity, an end to his letters, and still more irreparably an end to the visits to us in our own home, which by their length and increasing intimacy gave me much more to know, much more to venerate, and as time went on much more to love.

I never saw Housman again.

XXVI

When Christmas came I dispatched my usual Christmas letter. There was no reply. However great his aversion to correspondence, Housman was always scrupulously prompt in answering letters;

and when a week passed, and a second, and a third, and still no reply, I knew there must be something very seriously wrong. Waiting became more and more difficult, but I chose to go empty rather than pester him with inquiries, and I could think of no Cambridge friend who would be likely to have the information I wanted. So the waiting went on, and the increasing anxiety. At last a message came, a brief message on a postcard. It told me that he had just spent three weeks in the Nursing Home, unable to answer letters, that he was now back in College and lecturing, but his strength was barely sufficient for necessary work, so I must forgive this poor acknowledgment.

The possibility of showing something more than solicitude, of giving something more than sympathy – a desire and a hope, in short, of doing a friendly service, flashed across my mind the moment I laid the postcard down. Now that he had left the Nursing Home he would have to forgo many of its comforts and ministrations that mean so much to a chronic invalid. At best he would have many hours of loneliness – and it was the thought of a loneliness so little relieved by casual and uncertain visitors that moved me most deeply to compassion, and that seemed to offer the most promising chance for usefulness. The necessary work he spoke of, once accomplished with such ease and mastery, would, in his present state, be rather a measure of his declining vigour than a source of enlivenment; and when it was done, the hours of the long day still to be got through, and as they drew to a close the dread of sleeplessness, or of awaking to the suffocation that came with sleep, and no nurse at hand to administer the antidote.

I wrote at once. I offered to go to Cambridge at a day's notice, to serve in any capacity he wished, from that of occasional visitor – always and only at his bidding – to that of male nurse, for attendance night or day; and to remain as long as he found my services useful.

I waited, as once before, in a not dissimilar case, with a good deal of uneasiness. Either he might take my suggestion as a bit of imbecile impulsiveness, or possibly in his state of frayed nerves, as a gratuitous and far-fetched irrelevance. I had not long to wait; he must, I think, have written the first available moment. The letter was an unusually lengthy one for Housman, occupying four full sides of note-paper. It could not be called a gracious letter. It was mainly directed at my 'wrong-headedness'. But it was the swiftly-following letter that made atonement, and made it so simply, by casting off all disguises, and just revealing his hidden self.

It came in answer to a scribbled note in which I characterized his letter – mildly, I thought – as 'tart'.

He wrote:

> I am sorry to have written tartly: my intention was not so; and indeed the extreme and undeserved kindness and generosity of your letter moved me almost to tears.

I regretted at the time, and I have regretted and reproached myself to this day, that I did not go to see him again. If I had repeated the mild duplicity practised on the former occasion, pretended I had business in Cambridge on a given date, and told him how much I wished to seize the opportunity of calling for half an hour, I had not the smallest doubt of the answer he would make, or of the welcome he would give. Had a shadow of doubt crossed my mind, the memory of the last visit would have banished it. I hesitated, and in the end refrained, from a dread that compliance might be given solely for my satisfaction, without any regard for his own inclinations, or for the fret and worry a visit might cost him. He was not only seriously ill, and in a more advanced stage than on my former visit, but the nature of the illness was such as to render him peculiarly vulnerable to any disturbances of the customary quiet routine.

I decided he must not be troubled with proposals for a visit, and for the same reason delayed writing. But a brief note – his last – dated April 2nd, must have come in answer to a letter of mine. It was written in pencil. The writing was quite un-recognizable, many of the words could only be deciphered with difficulty, and the half-completed signature bore no resemblance to his own name, was vigorously scored out, and his own, incorrectly spelt, written firmly underneath. He tells me:

> My term was conducted to a triumphant end, but finally I had such bad nights that I was obliged to resort to the Nursing Home.

The letter goes on to say that, after two very wretched nights in the Home, he had been wondrously relieved by morphia and was now going on well.

That was the last I knew until, just a month later, the announcement of his death appeared in the newspapers.

*   *   *   *   *

In the loss of none other of my friends have I ever experienced such a sense of abruptness and desola-tion. There was no one to tell me that the end drew near, and no one to whom I could open my heart in condolence, or from whom I could seek relief to my solicitous questionings. In truth, the rest was silence.

I do not think any man could have gone so little out of his way to win affection as Housman; rather the contrary: he appeared neither to seek nor to expect affection; and when it came, and was beyond doubt, as in the case of R. V. Lawrence, he spoke of the acquisition, I vividly remember, with a naïveté that seemed to denote both an unusual occurrence and the intense pleasure it occasioned. If I am right in my conjecture that he purposely fought shy of giving or of awakening affection, it was assuredly not due to want of heart: no man, I am convinced, ever had more. It was and could only have been, that his excessive sensitiveness shrank from the possibility – to him it may have seemed the probability – of infidelity and disillusionment. He preferred to go without one of the most precious of this world's gifts rather than risk the pain of betrayal. It was this attitude perhaps that incited the flood of poetry in the nineties. Some outlet to his pent-up feelings must be found, and providentially the Muse was standing by to serve him.

When, one morning, in the visit before the last, disposed to intimacy as he had never before been, Housman told me he had never possessed but three friends – all, it is significant, associated with youth or early manhood. They were all now gone, and a note of exultation came into his voice as he spoke of his thankfulness for having outlived them. With a tenderness of passion utterly undisguised he went on to tell of the last of the three friends – a woman – recently dead. His voice faltered, his whole frame seemed shaken, as he told the brief story. He had loved and revered her from youth. In the earlier years companionship had been close and constant. Then distance and the exigencies of occupation had rendered meetings few and difficult, and of late years they had never met, he said bitterly, as a consequence of her having returned to her home-land, Germany, to end her days. The story closed with a thank God he had lived to know her safely laid to rest. He added – and for the first time his voice strengthened to a triumphant pitch – how comfortably he could meet death now his three friends were at peace.

In this deeply moving recital I particularly remarked a characteristic, more usual perhaps in women than in men, revealed on each of the two or three previous occasions when he indulged passionate utterance. His intensity of feeling was shown not by the use of emphatic words or declamatory expressions, but by the physical manifestations of a faltering voice, a flushed face, and an agitation of frame that gave the impression of a seething force restrained only by the exercise of stern self-discipline, and not always successfully, for a visible tremor would momentarily escape. All else, in contrast to his demeanour when he expatiated on the trials of the Senate House lecture, was under complete and destinate control — a low even tone, measured speech, and words the fewest and most tempered possible.

In a letter dated November 1934, in which he said that life was bearable, but he did not want it to continue, he referred to 'the great and real troubles of my early manhood'. What they were, and which was most effectual in misshaping his life in after days, can, it appears, only be conjectured. As I have already said, Housman's sister, Mrs. Symons, inferred that the lady I had mentioned in an article contributed to the *New Statesman and Nation*, must be a family friend, much his senior, to whom she knew he had given his boyish devotion, but a devotion, she also knew, that had passed with boyhood. Of his affection for the German lady Mrs. Symons knew nothing; she had not the smallest conception that any intercourse between them had survived the first casual meeting, neither had she supposed it had given birth to aught beyond a pleasant, mutually enjoyable relationship. This appears to be the first indication that the young Housman, who had hitherto been the life and soul of his family's enterprises, the acknowledged leader, of whom they were all proud, to whom they were all devoted, was already taking the lonely path that was to lead him away from them, away from other human intimacies, and steadily into an ever-deepening isolation.

The 'great and real troubles' of which he spoke were, in so acutely sensitive a disposition, the main factor doubtless, but to me it seemed certain that another influence had played a decisive part. The longer I knew him, and the more I saw him in contact with people, not his colleagues only, the more I felt his very gifts and attainments – his wide and exact knowledge, his faultless memory, his swift repartee and merciless tongue – were an added source of estrangement. The most of folk stood in awe of him, preserved silence, and encouraged silence in him. As a hindrance to the normal flow of intercourse what more effective illustration need be given than a remark he made at our own dinner table, in this case not a display of learning, merely of manner? He was telling us of a dining-club dinner at the house of one of its members, and of the unprecedented occurrence of the lady of the house sitting down with them at the meal. Worse followed: she positively had the audacity, he said, to await them in the drawing-room, and to stay there till her customary hour for retiring.

'Where would you have her be, if not in her own room?' asked another guest, mildly, in vindication of her sex.

'In the pantry!' he snapped.

It might have been said differently, and perhaps not less effectively. Instead, it was a brand he flung straight from the burning, and in consequence one voice was silenced for the remainder of the evening. And I am pretty sure that a similar usage, or the fear of it, was the cause of silence elsewhere, and on other occasions, and in other folk, in Housman's company. If only, I used often to think – if only we could all have handled him spontaneously, lightly, and unafraid, as my daughter did on that unforgettable evening when she brought another Housman to light, how great had been the gain to us, and to him maybe even greater!

By his own telling, he had never possessed but three friends, and all were then dead. If I dare to apply the term to him, and to call him friend, it is because, whatever he gave in return, his companionship won from me progressively those feelings that are alone and universally characteristic of friendship. Even so, I should apply the word with greater diffidence but for the fact, that, as time went on, his behaviour more and more encouraged, and at last I believe confirmed the claim. When I recall how willingly he renewed his visits, year by year, and insisted on paying the last of them, ill though he was, and broken, and just released from desperate symptoms; and when, still more convincingly, I recall the confidences he had reposed in me, and the look that accompanied them, and the look at many another time of converse – yes, I am satisfied of my right to call him friend; and it is as a friend I mourn his loss.